The Corricks,

Thanks for your

People !

PROFILES
IN
CHARACTER

PROFILES IN CHARACTER

BY

ROLFE CARAWAN

LIFEMATTERS
PRESS
Federal Way, Washington

Profiles in Character

ISBN   0-9651624-0-0

Library of Congress Cataloging-in-Publication # 96-94121

Copyright © 1996 by Rolfe Carawan. All rights reserved. No part
of this publication may be reproduced, stored in a retrieval system, or transmitted in any form or by any means — electronic,
mechanical, photocopy, recording, or any other — except for brief
quotations in printed reviews, without the prior written permis-
sion of the publisher.

DEDICATION

To Mom and Dad —

Thanks for the good start.

I hope to finish well.

ACKNOWLEDGMENTS

I am deeply grateful to some folks who contributed their time and talents to this book:

Karen Stimer — for her tireless research, excellent editing of my efforts, and the writing and rewriting of the manuscript. If you enjoy reading this book, Karen deserves much credit.

Ken Durham — for his valuable contributions to the profiles.

Chuck Haas — a great friend, for the creative genius behind the cover design.

Mark and Kathy Walker — for their friendship and encouragement.

Debbie Simmonds, Jean Rehberg and Ryan Rehberg — for their invaluable suggestions.

Lea — my incredible wife, for believing in me even when I did not believe in myself. Thank you, Sweetheart. I could not have done it without you.

TABLE OF CONTENTS

PROLOGUE
The Power of Character 3

AMBITION
Just Peanuts 9
The Man Who Would Be Everything 15

INTEGRITY
For Hearth and Home 25
The Choice of a Champion 29

COURAGE
The Madman and the Law 37
The Conductor 41

DUTY
America's Secret Weapons 49
A Soldier's Shame 53

DETERMINATION
What Does It Take to Make A Dream Happen? 61
Tenacity on the High Seas 67

EXCELLENCE
The "Real McCoy" 75
Of Socks and Success 79

PERSISTENCE

Skeeter's Triumph 87

Poor Tommy 91

MAGNANIMITY

The Heart That Healed a Nation 99

The Price of Poverty 103

DILIGENCE

The Making of a Maestro 111

What If? 117

COMPASSION

Where An Angel Dared to Tread 127

The Real Score 133

MORALITY

Through the Eyes of a Child 141

Lessons from Paradise 145

INDEX 151

PROLOGUE

THE POWER OF CHARACTER

What lies behind us and what lies before us are tiny matters compared to what lies within us.

THE POWER OF CHARACTER

Few have ever heard of her. To my knowledge, none have written about her. But every town has one like her — or should. A beacon of light. A refreshing drink to a parched soul. An example of life as it should be lived.

Everyone called her Miss Gladys. She was a devoted wife, mother, daughter and friend. And she was constitutionally incapable of saying "no" to anyone. As children, we couldn't wait to escape to Miss Gladys' house after school for pop and cookies! Not *milk* and cookies, but *pop* and cookies! Miss Gladys had two children of her own, but there were always more than that around her house. She was remarkable in her ability to make people feel welcomed and accepted.

As we navigated the rapids of adolescence, Miss Gladys was our guide and our encourager. Because of her open-door policy, we were free to discuss our fears, failures and frustrations. Yet she was no passive listener. She would listen carefully and attentively as we, in all our pubescent wisdom, loudly explained how we could make our own decisions regarding anything our hormones were screaming for at the moment. With greater wisdom and discernment, Miss Gladys would just smile affectionately, look us square in the eye and say, "Honey, I hear you; but you're wrong."

'She just needs more information,' we would conclude and launch into greater detail, explaining the obvious to her once again. In her slight Southern drawl, she would say, "Oh, now I understand! But you're still wrong!" Then she would sweetly explain how what we were wanting would hurt us, our families or someone else. She uncompromisingly told us the truth, even when we didn't like it. Though we sometimes ignored her advice (to our own loss, I might add), we always respected her example and willingness to set moral boundaries. Right was right and wrong was wrong with Miss Gladys. And we loved her because of her courage and conviction.

On Good Friday, 1981, Miss Gladys, her husband and another couple were returning from a golfing trip out of state. Passing through a small town in Virginia, they ran into construction delays near a railroad track. A flagman was directing the congested flow of automobiles along the two open lanes of the highway. He waved their car across the tracks, not realizing that traffic ahead was not moving. They were forced to stop, straddling the tracks, totally boxed in and unable to move. Then the awful clang of the warning bell pierced the air. From their right, a train was speeding toward them. Miss Gladys and her husband were on that side of the car, he in front and she in the back. He was able to jump from the car just before the impact, but Miss Gladys was not as quick. She had only one foot on the ground when the train slammed broadside into the car, knocking it over thirty yards away. Miss Gladys was crushed.

She was transported to Norfolk General Hospital, where she spent twenty-four days in intensive care. During her hospital stay a constant stream of people came by to inquire and pay their respects. Nearly every one pulled aside a family member to say, "You know, Miss Gladys loved everybody; but she really loved me best." Amazingly, that was true. She had a remarkable ability to make everyone believe she "loved them best."

The day after Mother's Day, Miss Gladys' candle gently flickered out. The little Baptist church in which she taught Sunday School for twenty years seated 500 people. It was standing room only the day of her funeral. Among those attending were two nurses from the Intensive Care Unit, come to pay their respects to a former patient — something they had never done before. Her funeral procession was the longest our little town had ever seen.

As I stood with the others at the graveside service, I was in awe of the number and variety of people brought together by this simple, humble woman. Young, old, black, white . . . she had touched them all.

I tried to identify exactly what it was about Miss Gladys that made her so special to so many. The answer was really more simple than I ever imagined. It was *who she was* that had touched these people, not just what she said or did. The strong yet gentle influence of her impeccable character had made a difference for us all.

As I watched them slowly lower Gladys Ruba Carawan, my mom, into the grave, I determined to make that kind of difference for others as well. I would do my best to develop the kind of inner strength that made her such an unforgettable and influential person.

My mom was the first "profile in character" to touch my life. She proved that character is "caught" as much as it is "taught" — that a life well-lived can be an infectious source of strength and hope and change for all it touches. So I began a search for other people whose lives offered rich examples of those character qualities so desperately needed in our families, our schools, our workplaces today. Following are just a few who have come to be my friends on this journey. They are just "profiles" — sketches or outlines of some of the qualities I want to have in my life. But they have inspired me to continue to choose right over wrong, good over evil, love over hate, kindness over apathy. My hope is that they will become your friends, too, and that their "profiles" would be fleshed out in your life just as they were in my mom's.

A M B I T I O N

He who sacrifices his conscience to ambition
burns a picture to obtain the ashes.

— Chinese proverb

JUST PEANUTS

If you travel down Main Street in Enterprise, Alabama, you will come across a rather puzzling monument. The legend reads, "In profound appreciation of the boll weevil and what it has done. . . . " Appreciation? To the boll weevil? Isn't that the ravenous insect that laid waste the great cotton fields of the South for twenty-five years? Why, Enterprise itself had been so devastated by the effects of the boll weevil that banks collapsed and stores went bankrupt. Yes, it is that same boll weevil. But the appreciation is not for the tragedy it brought, but the triumph it fostered . . . and not really for the insect itself, but for the man who showed the South the way out of the disaster.

George Washington Carver could not give you his exact date of birth. He did not even know who fathered him. As an infant, he and his mother were kidnapped from their owners by slave traders. George was released when a family friend caught up with the rogues and traded a horse for the sickly child, but he never saw his mother again. George nearly died several times as an infant, at one time coughing so violently that his vocal cords were torn. The damage to his voice would remain for a lifetime.

Too frail to work in the fields, George worked around the house of the generous Carver family and learned to cook, do laundry, iron clothes and sew. But what he liked to do best was to garden. He was fascinated with plants and how they grew. He would explore, experiment and learn all about every plant in his garden. His curiosity made him a quick learner. At the age of nine, he was known as the "plant doctor" for his ability to nurse sick plants and flowers back to health.

George's hunger to learn was insatiable. But the nearest school for black children was eight miles away. He knew that if he were to get an education, he would have to make his own way. So he left the only home he had ever known, armed only with his native intelligence and his domestic skills. To pay for his books and board, he worked as a family's "hired girl." He would rely on these household skills over the next fifteen years to pay for his schooling when financial resources were limited. It was the beginning of his education in learning to use what was available to him rather than complain about what he did not have. And it was a lesson that carried him all the way through college and his incredible career.

When he accepted a position years later to head up the agricultural department at the Tuskegee Institute in Tuskegee, Alabama, George was again faced with the problem of "non-existent" resources. He needed to set up an experimental lab. Gathering his prodigies around him, he picked up two balls of string. Holding up the hopelessly tangled ball he stated, "This is ignorance." Holding up the neatly wound ball he said, "This is intelligence."

The object lesson was not lost on his students. Nothing was to be wasted. Through creative effort and order, anything could be useful. If one man's trash is another man's treasure, then George Washington Carver was to be a wealthy man. There was plenty of trash to be found: The piles only needed to have intelligence applied to them. Again and again, his humble resourcefulness would save the day. An ink bottle, a cork and string became a Bunsen burner. Discarded bottles became beakers. Pieces of tin with holes of varying sizes punched in them became soil strainers. In short order, the students had created a lab and learned a most valuable lesson: Success can be achieved through intelligence and resourcefulness, regardless of "suitable" or elaborate means.

Which brings us back to the boll weevil. George had seen the pitiful condition of the soil in the South. He had foreseen the coming devastation, pleading with farmers to plow under their cotton and plant peanuts. George knew the peanut was an incredibly nutritious food source, capable of providing food for the farmers, replenishing the soil...and eradicating the boll weevil in the process. But his warnings went unheeded.

Then the destruction became too great. Reluctantly, farmers began to comply. Soon peanuts were the primary crop planted in the South. The harvest was plentiful. Too plentiful. There were more than enough peanuts to feed the people, but with no other practical use for them, many just rotted in the fields. Carver was devastated. How could he have been so shortsighted? The people needed a cash crop to replace the cotton. Could peanuts be that kind of crop as well? Could there be other uses for the peanut besides food?

During his daily pre-dawn walk in the woods, Carver's heart was broken. He turned to his source of inspiration and illumination. "Oh, Mr. Creator, why did you make the peanut?" Carver asked. He said later that the Lord Himself went back to the laboratory to work with him.

He locked himself away to learn the secrets of the peanut. Through heat and pressure he began splitting the oils from the starches, oils which could be used for cooking, margarine and even cosmetics. Enthusiastically, he focused on the meat and powder left as residue. A little water, some heat and out came peanut milk. Ice creams, cheeses and peanut butter soon followed! Turning to the paper-thin skin, he discovered thirty different dyes that would hold their color and be harmless to humans. The list would continue to grow until at his death, he had discovered over 300 uses for the peanut. Amazingly, this one crop alone could yield nearly everything man needed to survive. The tyranny of King Cotton was over!

What George Washington Carver did as a scientist was revolutionary. He took raw natural materials and found industrial uses for them, creating new products from their chemistry. He is recognized as the first "chemurgist," the man who literally opened the door to all the synthetics we enjoy today. But what George Washington Carver *was* as a human being was far more revolutionary. A deeply religious man, he stood in awe of the magnificent order and diversity he saw in all creation. His goal was to be the best steward of those riches he could possibly be. To his well-trained eye, everything had a purpose and nothing was to be wasted.

And he knew intuitively that what he was doing was not for himself alone. He believed passionately that he was called to help "the man farthest down" and that conviction became the driving force of his life. That is why Thomas Edison couldn't lure him away from his lab in Tuskegee with the promise of a six-figure income. That is why Henry Ford's offer of a job fell on deaf ears. Carver knew his place was in his lab at Tuskegee, exploring the riches of God's creation and releasing what God had placed there to help as many people as possible.

Though driven in his pursuit of nature's bounty, George Washington Carver's ambition was wonderfully tempered by this tremendous sense of humility. He exhibited it in sweeping floors and sewing on buttons to buy books for his schooling. He demonstrated it in the uncomplaining resourcefulness he showed in creating his own lab instruments at Tuskegee. He evidenced it in devoting his energies to the lowly peanut — a crop long disparaged by farmers and fed only to dogs — all to help raise the living standard of his fellow human beings.

That's why we don't really think he'd mind that the monument in Enterprise, Alabama, is to the boll weevil and not to him personally. He would probably have it no other way.

THE MAN WHO WOULD BE EVERYTHING

The waiting troops tried to quiet their nervous horses as they watched their companions cross the river
below and head back. The silence seeped into their
own bones and made involuntary shivers dance along
their spines. Something was wrong. Something was
very wrong.

The bright sun of that June morning in 1876
should have revealed the ordered ranks of blue cavalry uniforms along the river, awaiting the battle.
Instead, the hills were covered with unidentifiable
objects, some light and some dark. They were probably the carcasses of buffalo. An abandoned Indian
encampment nearby showed signs of a hurried depar-
ture — the Indians had probably left the animals in
their retreat.

The return of the scouts brought devastating
news. The objects scattered on the hillside across the
river were not dead buffalo but dead soldiers and
horses. Over two-hundred stripped bodies, pale in the
sunlight — their dead mounts beside them. Five

entire troops of one of the most famous Cavalry regi-
ments on the Plains lay strewn across the Montana
earth. Where was their leader? Where was the flam-
boyant "Yellow-Hair," the touted "Boy General" of
the Civil War and Indian campaigns? Where had
George Armstrong Custer's ambition brought him
this time?

Ambition had seemed to serve George well. It
secured him an appointment to West Point, an honor
usually reserved for well-to-do families who could
return the favor with political support. The son of a
Democratic blacksmith in Republican Ohio, he had
written to the senator charged with granting the
appointments, boldly confessing his true political lean-
ings and asking for the place anyway because he wanted to be a soldier. Impressed with the young man's
audacity, the senator gave him the next opening.

Getting to West Point was the key to everything for
young George. In the 1800s, West Point graduates
were almost guaranteed professional and social success.
They became the elite of the armed forces. They moved
in the highest social circles wherever they were stationed. They were ripe for post-service careers in business or politics. Among themselves they formed a network of mutual assistance that survived over lifetimes.
And with war over slavery looming on the horizon, the
young men of the class of 1862 would also find themselves on an even faster track to the glories of the battlefield and beyond. An entire new world opened up to
George with that West Point appointment.

His West Point career didn't mark him as a stand-out, however. He finished thirty-fourth in a class of thirty-four. Graduating one full year early because of the opening of the Civil War, George was poised with his classmates to ship off to Washington to begin his career in the Union Army. But less than one week out of the academy, he was arrested for failing to prevent a fight between cadets on the campus and was scheduled for court-martial. However, his former classmates prevailed on superiors in Washington and he was ordered released with only a reprimand. It would not be the first time in his military career that he would be arrested and reprieved by others who wanted his services. But it did mark the beginning of the famous "Custer luck" that seemed to follow him everywhere.

If his West Point career had been lackluster, his Civil War career was brilliant. It was not because of his superior strategy or skills, but mostly because he was in the right place at the right time with the right people watching. Though all his classmates benefited from the accelerated promotion schedule of wartime, Custer rocketed far beyond them all. Within two years, he was made a Brigadier General, the youngest man in U.S. history to be so honored.

His bold impulsiveness and irresistible charm continued to bring him success after success. Superiors tolerated him because he got the job done, but the enlisted men loved him because he was not like any other officer with whom they had ever served. He shared their inconveniences out in the field. He did his best to secure the finest provisions for them. He flaunted convention by devising his own uniform — a velveteen jacket with gold trim, boots above the knee, a soft hat and a bright red scarf around his neck. He gathered all sorts of pet animals around him, sleeping with them in his tent. And there was always the hair — sometimes cut short and scented with cinnamon oil, but more often allowed to grow and hang in soft golden curls on his shoulders. Somehow, he managed to be the center of attention wherever he was.

But his career had its dark side. More than once, he brashly disobeyed direct orders in the field and took his men into impossible situations. His charges into enemy territory were bold and brought him much notoriety, but they were also bloody. He lost more men than almost any other commander in the Civil War. The "Boy General" never seemed to be able to curb his compulsive drive for fame — and others paid the price for it.

Perhaps that reputation preceded him as his career turned westward after the war. By the time Custer arrived at Ft. Lincoln in North Dakota almost twelve years later, his various commands had been marked by tense hostility from fellow officers and massive desertions among the enlisted men. Only the civilian press and those closest to him continued to fawn over him. Though the famous "Custer luck" was still holding and he was recognized as the greatest Indian fighter on the Plains, many were growing increasingly wary of his decisions.

That spring of 1876 was supposed to be the crowning moment. For months, Indians and whites had both known that the battles of those spring expeditions would be defining ones. For months, forts throughout the Plains had been making preparations for a final, forcible relocation of Indians to the reservations. For those same months, Indians had been gathering near the Little Bighorn River in Montana territory, leaving their agencies and reservations in droves to unite under Sitting Bull for one last thrust against the white man.

As Custer moved his men west in search of the Indian camp on June 24, 1876, he must have been thinking about the timing of it all. Succeeding here would open as many new doors to him as the appointment to West Point had done nearly twenty years before. The country's centennial was less than two weeks away. How glorious to return to Washington as the man who succeeded in defeating the Sioux once and for all! And the Democratic presidential convention was due to start in just three days. News of a Custer victory in Montana might create a ground swell of adulation that could even sweep him into the White House. What a fitting climax to the career of this ambitious son of a Democratic blacksmith from Republican Ohio!

Coming upon the Indian camp a full day before he was to meet up with two other generals and their cavalries, and ignoring his scouts' warnings about the number of braves before him, Custer made the typical decision to attack immediately. Boldness and surprise had always worked in his favor before. Why should it be any different now? And if victory were to come (and he never doubted it would), it would be his and his alone. He had every confidence that they would finish the job and be heading back home before the day was over.

He split his exhausted men into three groups, relying on the same tactics that had brought him such mixed results in the Civil War. One group was attacked almost immediately and forced to withdraw into the rocks and cottonwoods. Deciding to retreat to a nearby hill where he could maintain higher ground and wait for his third group to come to his aid, Custer and his men found themselves fighting hand-to-hand with more Indians than they had ever seen. Inch by hard-fought inch they were ascending the hill, when the impossible happened. Hundreds of Indians appeared above them, having patiently waited for just that move. In less than twenty minutes, the battle was over. The famous "Custer luck" had finally run out. The boldness had finally been revealed as folly. And the battle that was to usher the golden-haired "Boy General" into immortal greatness would come to be known as "Custer's Last Stand." Ambition had consumed its host.

REFLECTIONS ON AMBITION...

Its original Latin meaning was "going around." In Rome, candidates for public office would "go around" soliciting votes. Quite possibly because of the type of men who were associated with it, the word became synonymous with a desire for a position, for honor or power.

Ambition itself is not necessarily a problem. Without a drive to improve, to succeed, to go forward, life becomes safe and stale. Progress ceases. Comfortableness can easily become a coffin of the spirit.

The *scope* of ambition is critical, however. When the aim is broad, including the genuine welfare of others, incredible things can happen. George Washington Carver's desire to help "the man farthest down" was that kind of ambition. Coupled with a deep sense of humility, ambition drove him to exhaust all the possibilities of the lowly peanut in order to help as many others as he possibly could.

But when the aim is constricted and focused

on self alone, ambition becomes myopic and all-consuming. It can even become deadly. You have only to look at that Montana hillside to grasp the difference.

Go ahead and set your sights high. Aim for the top. Don't ever be content with mediocrity and the status quo. But always be sure that your sights don't run through other people, that your aim is other- and not self-centered, and that what you desire will not corrupt you in the process. Remember these two men named George . . . and choose your ambitions wisely.

INTEGRITY

*A reputation once broken may possibly be repaired,
but the world will always keep their eyes on the
spot where the crack was.*

— Joseph Hall

FOR HEARTH AND HOME

Mary sat pondering what her husband would do. The house was quiet except for the sound of his pacing in the bedroom overhead. Back and forth he went for hours. She knew that the decision facing him was sheer agony. A man of deep convictions, Robert had an uncompromising sense of honor and duty. Now these two character traits were at virtual war with each other. The battle raging within him was tearing at the very fiber of his soul. Mary heard a loud thud, as if someone was falling to the floor. Alarmed, she strained to hear if he was all right. She detected a faint voice and knew what was going on. Robert had once again dropped to his knees to pray for guidance. She knew he would have an answer soon.

The next morning, April 21, 1861, Robert quietly walked over to his wife with a letter in hand and said, "Well, Mary, the question is settled." After thirty-two years of faithful service in the United States Army (soon to be called the "Union Army"), Robert E. Lee was handing in his letter of resignation.

The battle that had just been waged in his soul was about to spill over into the War Between the States, a conflict that would claim over 600,000 lives in four years. Few today can understand how a man of such great honor and conviction could choose to side with a rebellion that supported the slavery of human beings. The answer lay deep within the core of the man. Though he was proud to be an American, Robert E. Lee was first and foremost a Virginian. Family roots and regional loyalties were deeply felt in the still-young nation. As the son of Revolutionary War hero "Light-Horse" Harry Lee, Robert's primary affections had always been directed toward his home state of Virginia. The truth was, Robert despised the idea of secession as much as he did the institution of slavery. But those issues paled for him in the light of what he called "hearth and home." Were he to remain a soldier of the Union army and were Virginia to join the rebels in seceding from the Union, he would be forced to take up arms against his own flesh and blood, perhaps even members of his own family. This he simply could not do. Hearth and home were of more value to him than his commission in the army. So he left the lifetime of military service he had carefully built to remain with his family.

Before too long, Robert E. Lee was commissioned a General in the newly formed Confederate Army. Though badly outnumbered, Lee won most of his early battles, due in part to his tactical brilliance. But an even greater factor, especially as the war dragged on, was the unbridled devotion of the men to Lee himself. Some men have the financial ability to buy devotion. Others demand it by their position of authority. Lee was one of the rarest of all leaders: He earned it. His every thought was for the welfare of the men under his command. Every hardship they suffered, he suffered. If they went cold and hungry, he went cold and hungry. Every battle plan he implemented was devised with the goal of saving as many lives as possible. He loved his men and his men loved him...and followed him to the very end.

The end came on April 9, 1865, in the McLean house in Appomattox, Virginia. It had been nearly four years to the day since Lee had wrestled through that sleepless night of decision. Though he hated the thought of surrender, devotion to "hearth and home" once again compelled him to act. He knew that surrender was the only way to spare all of his countrymen more needless bloodshed.

He rose early that April morning and put on his finest uniform. He wore his best polished boots and buckled on his dress sword. If he was going to become General Grant's prisoner, he would be an honorable-looking prisoner.

During the ceremonies, as always, his concern for his men drove his actions. Under the proposed terms of surrender, Lee and his army would not be imprisoned if they took an oath to not fight again. His officers, but not the enlisted men, could keep their weapons and horses. Lee hesitated. He then pointed out to General Grant that the cavalry men and gunners had also used their own horses in the war. To give them up now meant the men would have no animals to work the land when they returned home. With an assurance from Grant that enlisted men as well as officers could keep their animals, Lee signed the surrender, as dignified in defeat as he was in victory.

Robert E. Lee stands as a shining example of what a leader should be: loyal, honorable, dignified. He was more concerned for those under his charge than for himself. And above all, he was true to himself. In choosing *principle* over *position,* Lee marked himself as a man of unswerving character and integrity.

However, he paid a high price to follow his convictions. Possibly his greatest loss was his beloved plantation in Arlington, Virginia, overlooking Washington, D.C. It was part of the "hearth and home" for which he had been willing to fight. Confiscated by the U.S. government and used as a hospital for Union soldiers during the war, it was never returned to his family. Its final disposition, however, is somehow fitting to the man who once called it home. Today it is a memorial to the honor, integrity and self-sacrifice that have marked succeeding generations of men just like Robert E. Lee. He called it his Curtis-Lee Mansion. We call it Arlington National Cemetery.

THE CHOICE OF A CHAMPION

The team masseur watched the young runner make his final preparations. The sweltering July heat made the challenge before him seem more than impossible. Oh, he had trained hard and well — but changing your race from the 100-meter to the 400-meter this close to the actual competition was almost unheard of. And these were the Olympics! As they left the hotel, the masseur pressed a folded-up note into the young man's hand. With a gracious smile, the athlete said he would read it at the stadium. The masseur didn't know if his young charge could win the race, but he did know that the Scottish runner walking out the door had heart. And if heart could win a race, then maybe he stood a chance.

Eric Liddell was well known in his native Scotland by 1924. His family and friends knew him as a better athlete than student, always fair and sportsmanlike in his conduct, but always running to win. He had been known to share his trowel with a competitor to help him dig out a "foot hole" for a better start . . . to loan his coat to another before a race so "he wouldn't be stiff"... to give up the better inside position and take the outside position in a race because his opponent was less experienced. For years, many had known him as "The Flying Scotsman"... the best up-and-coming sprinter in the country... Britain's best hope for a gold medal in the 100-meter dash at the upcoming Olympics. They *knew* he would win. Perhaps that is why what he did seemed like such a betrayal.

The 1924 Olympics were held at Paris' Columbus Stadium. All eyes were fixed on Eric's race: the 100-meter dash. Everyone was anticipating the young Scottish man with the unorthodox running style to break the tape once more and set a new record. Then came the blow. When he learned that the qualifying heats were to be run on a Sunday, Eric Liddell made a quiet but definitive statement: "I'm not running on a Sunday." The British Olympic Committee members were aghast. This was the opportunity of a lifetime! He could be famous — his name immortalized! He could bring honor to himself and his country! What was he possibly thinking?

He was thinking of the Commandment he had known from his childhood: that the Sabbath was to be kept holy. It was something he had never violated in his competitive career to that point and did not intend to violate — no matter the race. The world had long known that *losing* was not in his vocabulary: They now learned that *compromise* wasn't either. And they were brutally unforgiving.

Though he cheered long and hard as his fellow Brit, Harold Abrahams, won the 100-meter dash, and though he himself placed third for the bronze in the 200-meter race, he was all but ignored by the press. He had not run the event the world had waited to see him run. He had let them all down. He was a traitor to them all.

As he prepared to take the track for the 400-meter finals, Eric remembered the note from the masseur. He read it — and a smile broke across his face. Assurance and confidence filled his heart. The note simply read: "In the Old Book it says, 'He that honors me, I will honor.' Wishing you the best of success always."

In typical fashion, Eric went down the line before the race to shake each opponent's hand. He may have been saying "good-bye," because once the gun sounded, they never saw his face again! Eric sprinted all out to take a commanding lead at the 200-meter mark. It was to be expected: This was simply the 200-meter man giving his best at the first. They all knew that he would "blow up" at the end. No one could maintain that pace for 400 meters. Sure enough, the American Harold Fitch (who had just set a new world record in the event) pulled within two meters. Then the unbelievable happened. As if fighting for his life, the "Flying Scotsman" began his flailing, unconventional style of running. Clawing the air with windmill-like arm strokes, kicking his knees almost into his chest, gasping for air with every breath, Eric started to pull away. He broke the tape with a new world record of 47.6 seconds.

The crowd erupted. Those who had so recently branded him a traitor now hailed him as a hero. He had done it! He had won! Few understood that the real victory had not been won on the racetrack, but days before in Eric's own heart. The medal was not the reward: The integrity he showed was the real prize.

Faster...higher...stronger had been the motto of the 1924 Olympics. Without a doubt, Eric had been faster. But he had also gone higher and become stronger because he didn't compromise his beliefs in his pursuit of excellence. He refused the temptation to rationalize, to short-cut, to make exceptions for temporary gain. He chose *principle* over *prestige*...and became a champion in life, not just in the Olympics.

REFLECTIONS ON INTEGRITY...

We immediately make the connection to *honesty* when we speak of *integrity:* saying what we mean, keeping our word, following through on promises. A person of integrity *does* what he *says* he will do.

But this emphasis on the verbal aspect ignores a larger perspective. At its root, the word means "whole; entire; complete; undivided." Remember *integers* in elementary math — whole numbers as opposed to fractions?

A person of integrity is *whole* in the way he lives his life. He isn't fractured or divided by competing loyalties or codes. There is a distinct absence of deceit, fraud or hypocrisy about him. He doesn't claim principles he fails to operate by. He doesn't act one way in public and another in private. He doesn't just "talk the talk." He "walks the walk."

Integrity prevented Robert E. Lee from taking up arms against his own flesh and blood. Integrity made it impossible for Eric Liddell to run on a Sunday. They could do nothing else without violating their own moral principles, without dividing their loyalties, without compromising their own internal sense of rightness.

In these two men, belief and behavior were brought together in one seamless whole — entire, complete and undivided. They show us the genuineness and authenticity that can only come from living from the inside out — operating by a core set of principles that does not change with circumstance or emotion.

Integrity. It even sounds solid, doesn't it?

COURAGE

Courage is almost a contradiction in terms.
It means a strong desire to live taking
the form of a readiness to die.

— G. K. Chesterton

THE MADMAN AND THE LAW

He was the most hated and vilified congressman of his time — a stubborn, ill-humored old man who delighted in agitating his peers. During his time in office, Monday was the official petition day in the House of Representatives. On that day, any member of the House could introduce petitions to the membership for consideration. And every Monday morning, his fellow congressmen entered the chamber with a feeling of great dread. If they spotted the shiny bald head of this rookie legislator in seat 203 of the House, they knew they were in for a very long day. It seemed he always came in with the same set jaw, the same determined look. And when he stood to speak, it was always about the same thing: "that abominable law," as he put it. At one point, it was reported that he had introduced 900 petitions against it — in one day! One of his fellow congressmen called him a "mischievous, bad old man" and some newspapers dubbed him the "madman of Massachusetts."

Who was this divisive troublemaker? Who was this

rabble-rouser who dared to speak against a law that had been legitimized by every government since 1787? He was John Quincy Adams; and his courageous battle against slavery provoked some of the most explosive showdowns and outrageous maneuvers in Congressional history. His stand was all the more noteworthy because he didn't have to take it at all. His reputation and his place in history were already secured. As the sixth President of the United States, he was entitled to retire to a life of reflective ease. But when his neighbors approached him in 1830 to run as their Congressman after his loss to Andrew Jackson, he accepted the honor and was handily elected. And so he arrived back in Washington, D.C., as a 63-year-old freshman congressman, beginning perhaps the greatest struggle of his political life.

As early as 1820, Adams had been engaged in the growing controversy over slavery. He had publicly spoken against it on moral grounds in debates with John C. Calhoun, all the while hoping a more articulate spokesman would take up the cause. But in the House of Representatives in 1830, there was no more articulate spokesman to be found than Adams himself; and he took his place with a tremendous sense of duty and purpose.

By 1836, some Southern Congressmen had had enough. Voting 117 to 68, they passed a gag rule that tabled all petitions relating to slavery, allowing no discussion whatsoever, much less referral to committee for action. For the next eight years, continuing gag rules were adopted. And during those eight years, Adams continued to present his petitions, using every bit of expertise and cunning his forty years in politics had given him. He managed to get the substance of each petition before the House without actually presenting the petition itself, artfully asking if a petition stating "such and such" would be against "the rule." His daily battle to repeal the gag rules infuriated his opponents as much as his stand against slavery. He could never rise to his feet to speak without enduring a jarring round of ridicule, repeated motions of censure and loud calls for his expulsion. But his courage never flagged. He remained a constant irritant to the status quo, a constant prod to the slow of conscience, a constant reminder of the immorality and illogic of men owning men, a constant voice for those he represented.

Finally, in 1844, the twenty-first gag rule was repealed. Adams had won the right to continue to petition against slavery. By that time, even his enemies acknowledged his courage and integrity. They called him "Old Man Eloquent." He died in 1846 after collapsing at his desk in the House, never having seen the abolition of the law he so despised.

While he accomplished many other great things in his career, John Quincy Adams' prolonged battle in Congress to abolish slavery has marked him perhaps even more than his Presidency as a man of unflagging moral courage. He dared to speak out when it was neither comfortable nor safe to do so. He dared to speak out when his personal reputation and safety were threatened. And he continued to speak out when there seemed to be no hope that he would ever be heard. That is the essence of courage — doing what is right simply because it is right to do so.

The Conductor

Heading north under the light of a full moon made the journey easier. At least they could see their way through the swamps. But that meant they could also be seen by others; so they hunched close to the surface of the brackish water, stepping carefully to diminish the splash of their movements. This group of fugitives had already learned a lot about hiding. They had learned to avoid the main roads, using rivers and wetlands to cover their footprints and confuse the bloodhounds tracking them. They traveled only at night, spending the daylight hours in whatever friendly houses, barns or fields were open to them. They had no real idea where they were at any given moment — they only knew where they were going and that it was worth any price to get there.

It was a journey thousands of others dreamed of taking. They knew they could lose their lives; but they weren't lives they wished to keep anyway. Many of them had been cruelly beaten or branded for identification purposes. They had been separated from their families and sold like stock animals. They had been humiliated, worked to exhaustion, deprived of hope and humanity. These were the slaves of nineteenth century America — and they wanted their freedom. So they boarded the "Underground Railroad" for the harrowing journey north. But this was a railroad unlike any other. Its tracks existed only in the minds of its conductors. Its depots were never identified by signs or distance markers. And its tickets were purchased by pure courage. The conductor on this particular trip was called "The General" and she had never lost a passenger on any of her runs. Her name was Harriet Tubman.

Harriet knew the stories of her passengers without hearing them. Born a slave in Maryland, she was quite familiar with their tales of physical and emotional abuse. She herself had been brutally attacked by her master, suffering a head wound that would cause her blackouts for the rest of her life. One day, she heard the news every slave feared the most: She and her family were to be sold "South." Being sent into the deep South was tantamount to a death sentence. The South used up everyone it received. To be in your forties there was to be an "Old Joe."

Then Harriet heard rumors of a way of escape. Quiet whispers fearfully shared in the fields and work shacks told of a network of houses, tunnels and roads — an "underground railroad" that led to freedom in the north for those willing to risk the journey. Her heart pounded. She had to try it. She had lived with the humiliation and despair long enough. She would not go South to die.

With only the North Star as her guide, Harriet eventually made it to Pennsylvania and freedom. She found work as a maid and began to experience the incredible joys of independence. She could, for the first time in her twenty-eight years, look forward to each new day. She no longer needed to feel the humiliation, the fear, the anger of slavery. But for some reason, she still did. A woman of deep compassion and conviction, her conscience would not give her rest as she thought about her family and friends still in Maryland, still bound by all the chains she had so recently cast off. She had to bring them out. She couldn't let them stay there any longer. So Harriet Tubman joined the ranks of the "conductors" on the Underground Railroad.

The courage this took is astounding. Escaped slaves received no mercy. Professional slave hunters prowled the countryside looking for "runaways." If found, she could be returned to her former owner, who could punish her as he saw fit. But her heart gave her no rest. She had to go.

Her first trip was perhaps the hardest — back to Maryland to rescue her sister and her sister's children. But other trips soon followed. She became extremely clever in organizing her journeys and evading suspicion. When her name and picture appeared on wanted posters for a $40,000 reward, she began to disguise herself as an old woman, dirty, disheveled and dressed in rags. She would shuffle along the streets and roads of the South, muttering to herself and singing familiar spiritual songs — a harmless old slave woman of no use to anyone anymore. The songs, however, were secret codes passing on information to potential passengers about her arrival and instructions for their escape. In fifteen years, Harriet made nineteen trips on the Underground Railroad and brought over 300 slaves to freedom.

There were many other conductors on this railroad to freedom, many of them former slaves themselves, all of them brave and selfless; but Harriet Tubman's name is nearly always mentioned first when the stories are told. Called "the Moses of her people," she stands as a symbol of all that we know about courage and bravery. Having achieved her life's dream, she willingly risked it that others might taste freedom as well. This tiny slip of a woman with the heart of a lion and the cunning of a fox is surely a heroine for all time.

REFLECTIONS ON COURAGE . . .

The word itself means "great heart." We usually associate it with the dramatic, split-second decisions to act in dangerous or extraordinary circumstances — the bystander plunging into an icy river to rescue a child, the Chinese student standing his ground in front of an army tank, the helicopter pilot rescuing a downed airman behind enemy lines. And we shake our heads and admit, "I couldn't do that. I'm not that brave."

But there are no fearless people. We all have things that make our palms sweat and our hearts race. Some simply learn to overcome their fears and do what needs to be done. Harriet Tubman and John Adams both show us this aspect of bravery: counting the cost, embracing the risk, and acting anyway because it is right to do so.

We cannot always wait for our palms to dry and our hearts to slow — some situations demand immediate action. But most of us will face only those circumstances that require this settled, determined brand of courage, exercised over the course of time — the decision to keep on doing what is right no matter what our fears are telling us. Resisting and mastering our fears — that is the kind of courage that can make "great hearts" of us all.

D U T Y

*A man has honour if he holds himself to an
ideal of conduct though it is inconvenient,
unprofitable or dangerous to do so.*

— Walter Lippman

AMERICA'S SECRET WEAPONS

Iwo Jima is a barren volcanic island in the South Pacific measuring a little less than eight square miles. A mere pin dot on the globe, it was the site of one of the costliest and most strategic battles in all of World War II. The month-long struggle for the island was heralded in a now-famous photo of U.S. Marines raising the flag on one of its peaks. Perhaps not as well known is the part some special secret weapons played in the ultimate success of the American troops on Iwo.

Developed quietly in the deserts of the American Southwest, these secret weapons did not involve superior firepower, expensive machinery or state-of-the-art technology. They were the brainchild of a man without any formal training in military strategy or tactics — Philip Johnston, son of missionaries. In fact, when he first suggested the use of the weapons to the Marine Corps in early 1942, he was met with total skepticism. But once the generals saw Johnston's idea in practice, they became enthusiastic supporters. Here were weapons that far outstripped anything the military had available at that moment. They were functional within minutes of delivery to troops in the field. They never went down due to "technical bugs." They were versatile, self-propelled and extremely resilient under battlefield conditions. In short, they were what they had always been and what Johnston knew them to be from his childhood — tough-minded, resolute, dependable Navajo Indians!

Known throughout the military as the "Navajo code-talkers," these incredible people were the secret weapons that literally turned the tide of the war in the Pacific. Their invaluable payload was their unique language. It proved to be the ultimate unbreakable code as the Allied troops hopscotched their way across the islands.

The Navajo language is practically incomprehensible to outsiders. With no alphabet or written symbols, it is totally dependent on vocal inflection and pitch for meaning. The only way to learn it is to hear it. Perhaps that is why it was the only native American language German experts did not study as part of their preparations for war. It remained unknown to Axis cryptographers even after peace was won.

The code developed by the Navajo units had only 411 words, most of them based on simple visual association. With no native word for "submarine," the code-talkers used *besh-lo*, literally "iron fish." An aircraft carrier was a *tsidi-ney-ye-hi*, or "bird carrier." A hand grenade was a "potato," a bomb was an "egg," and so on. There was also a code for individual letters in the event a word had to be spelled out, with the most common letters carrying several alternatives, just to add to the fun. The result was a "language" known only to the 400 or so Navajos themselves: Not even their American companions could follow its structure or vocabulary. It gave the Allies the capability of rapid-fire radio transmissions that, with a Navajo at each end, could be encoded and decoded within minutes without fear of interception or deciphering by the enemy.

But the importance of the Navajos didn't end with their role as radio operators. Though they were a common and treasured sight across the Pacific, hunched carefully over the radio transmitters they often hooked up under coconut trees for stability, they did so much more. These quietly dependable soldiers took up rifles when fighting was required, tools when building was required and shovels when digging in was required. They served with distinction and valor wherever they went. And when the campaign in the Pacific boiled down to that one pivotal battle on the barren rock of Iwo Jima, even the Marines acknowledged that the U.S. would not have taken the island without the Navajos.

Following the war, any of the code-talkers could have sought personal fame for the crucial part they played. But they didn't. They chose instead to keep their role and the unique code they had developed shrouded in secrecy. Why? They wanted to be ready should their country need their services again.

They maintained their silence for nearly twenty-five years. In 1969, one of the Marine divisions involved in the Pacific war publicly honored the code talkers. Two years later, then-President Richard Nixon appeared at a code-talker reunion to thank the men for their "resourcefulness, tenacity, integrity and courage." It was a tribute they had long deserved. Their deep sense of duty, pure and simple, honors them to this day.

A Soldier's Shame

The humiliation was almost too great to bear. He was a soldier and proud of it. He had promised to fight to the death, to never surrender. Just one moment of inattention... one slight relaxation of the watchfulness that had become second nature to him... and the damage had been done. There he stood, hands bound behind his back, guns pointed at his head. He had been taken prisoner. His guilt was overwhelming.

He remembered the day the enemy invaded the island in overwhelming numbers. He could still see his comrades dying valiantly around him. He and seven other survivors had headed into the dense jungle, planning to regroup and fight again. But without weapons, cut off from communication with other units of their army, their only fight was for survival in the jungle. All they could do was try to elude capture for as long as possible. Their commitment to duty and honor demanded no less.

Soon, only three were still alive. Then tempers

flared, and his two comrades moved a distance away. It seemed only a short time later that he discovered their bodies in a cave. He was finally and totally alone.

But the call to duty still burned within him. He continued to make every effort to remain hidden, always covering his footprints when he left his cave. He carefully chose his food, watching what the island animals ate before trying it himself. He boiled his own water and made his own medicines. A professional tailor before he became a soldier, he wove his own cloth from tree bark and made needles from the ammunition shells that littered the island. With his sense of duty driving him on, he did whatever he had to do to live up to his promise to his country. His entire focus was to keep himself mentally alert and physically ready for a return to duty. He could do no less.

And so he kept his word — until that terrible day when he was abruptly discovered by two other islanders also searching for food. Preoccupied, he hadn't heard the men until it was too late. Though he struggled bravely and nearly seized a pistol to use in his defense, he was taken down, bound and led away. Captured. And the shame was hot within him.

Thus it was on January 24, 1972 — some *twenty-eight years* after he first fled into the jungles during the U.S. invasion of Guam — Private Yokoi Shoichi of the Imperial Japanese Army unwillingly ended his quest to keep the commitment he had made as a young man in his twenties.

The public found his story incredible, almost

beyond belief. Even veteran soldiers could not imagine that a man would so honor his vows of service as to spend nearly three decades hiding in the jungle, living a life of self-imposed solitary confinement in a cave. Yet when Yokoi finally returned to his homeland, it was the commitment to duty that was still burning in his mind.

As he stepped off the plane at Haneda International Airport in Tokyo, the world waited to hear what this ultimate hero might have to say. Would he be overjoyed at his return to civilization, to family and friends left behind so long ago? Would he be bitter at what he had missed all those years? Would he finally feel relieved of the burden of wartime promises made under cultural conditions that had changed so dramatically? When he finally spoke, it was none of those things. He could only confess his deep sense of shame. He could only apologize for not keeping his word, for failing in his duty.

Time and changing ideologies have made Private Soichi's sense of duty seem excessive and unreasonable. Twenty-eight years in a cave because of a promise? Regardless of how we might disagree with the politics behind his commitment, there is an undeniable sense of honor surrounding this man who refused to break his word and shirk his duty as he understood it, no matter what it cost him. It is a sense of honor we find sadly lacking today.

REFLECTIONS ON DUTY...

Remember a time when a man's word was all that was needed to initiate and finalize a business deal? When marriages were made without pre-nuptial agreements and managed to last thirty, forty, fifty years as the norm? When a promise was a serious thing and a commitment didn't stop being a commitment because circumstances made it more difficult to keep?

But that was then, as they say, and this is now. A person's word and a person's duty are concepts rapidly disappearing from our world today. We are almost forced to look to times of crisis — like war — and to highly disciplined and organized segments of our culture — like the military — to recapture the idea. Navajo Indians who served with little notice and no recognition until years after their service and a Japanese soldier resolutely keeping faith with his promises seem to have so little to do with life in the twilight of the twentieth century.

While we might dismiss their deeds as "outdated" for our more enlightened day and age, there can be no question that a stronger sense of obligation to promises made would revolutionize our relationships and energize our societies. Far from limiting our personal freedoms, such an attitude would free us to relate to one another in a climate of honesty, trust and simplicity. How different our businesses, our professional associations, our politics, even our marriages and families would be with a resurrected sense of duty and commitment. Could that be the real lesson we need to learn from an incredible secret code and twenty-eight lonely years in a cave?

DETERMINATION

Consider the postage stamp: Its usefulness
consists in the ability to stick to
one thing till it gets there.

— Josh Billings

What Does it Take to Make a Dream Happen?

It looks like any other college campus: dormitories, classroom buildings, administration facilities. Though not as large as some, there is no doubt this is a place where learning occurs. No one would ever guess that it all began with a dream in the heart of a little African-American girl in Mayesville, South Carolina.

Mary McLeod was the fifteenth of seventeen children born to freed slaves Sam and Patsy McLeod and the first to have been born free on their own land. It was on a visit to the home of her parents' former owners that Mary felt the first stirrings of her dream. When the granddaughter invited Mary to look at her new playthings, Mary admired the dolls and toys, but felt her eyes continually drawn to a book on the table. Shyly picking it up, she turned the pages and wondered at the strange markings that covered the paper. Her curiosity was interrupted by a curt command: "Put that down! You know black children can't read!

Come here and I'll show you some pictures in this book instead!"

Mary put the book down, but she couldn't put down the questions that arose in her mind. Why couldn't she read? Why couldn't she learn just like other children had? Why weren't there any schools for her to go to like her white friends?

"God, please help me," she breathed. "Someday, I'm going to learn to read." And so the dream was born.

A year later, Miss Emma Wilson appeared in Mayesville as if in answer to this one child's prayer. The Presbyterian Church was going to open a school for black children and Miss Wilson wanted to invite the McLeod children to attend. Recognizing that there was something special within their daughter, Sam and Patsy excused her from the backbreaking work in the fields and sent her to school.

For four years, Mary walked five miles each way to attend Miss Wilson's school. She learned to read and do math. Every day she would repeat the lessons she had learned in school to her family members. As what she was learning in school became known in the area, neighbors came to her for help in making sure their accounts were figured correctly by the gin owners and the storekeepers. Graduation day was both joyous and disheartening. She had learned so much — and there was so much more she wanted to know. But there was no place to go. There were no other schools for black children in the area. And even if there had been schools, her family could not afford tuition for her to go. At eleven years of age, it appeared that Mary had reached the end of her dream.

But another Mary in another part of the country was dreaming as well. An older Mary, a white Quaker seamstress in Denver, Colorado, was consumed with the needs of the children of the recently freed slaves throughout the South. She had heard of Miss Emma Wilson's work and wanted to help. So Mary Chrissman underwrote a scholarship for one young black student of the school's choice. Her only condition was that the student be one who would "make good."

Miss Wilson didn't have to think twice about that choice. A year after her dream had seemed dead, Mary found herself on an eight-hour train trip from Mayesville to Concord, N.C. — a newly enrolled student at the Scotia Seminary. It would be more than seven years before Mary returned home to Mayesville to teach in her old school with her beloved Miss Wilson. By that time, Mary realized that her dream was taking on a new shape — she wanted to start a school of her own.

Marriage and the birth of a son intervened, but the new Mrs. Mary McLeod Bethune could not let her dream go. The hunger was the same as that of the little girl in the playroom so many years ago. She heard that people from all over the South were congregating in Daytona to build the Florida East Coast Railroad. She listened to reports of the horrible living conditions and the hundreds of children without adequate supervision or schooling. It became a magnet to her soul. In 1904, Mary arrived in Daytona, Florida, with $1.50 in her purse, her son in her arms, and the dream still burning in her heart.

She rented a broken-down, five-room house for $11 a month and began to make her dream happen. She recruited volunteers, solicited money and gathered supplies from whoever would listen to her, ignoring every social barrier she encountered. She sorted through the discards of the many hotels in Daytona, furnishing her school with lamps, boxes, crates, dishes and utensils thrown out as "unusable" by their staffs. Her desk was a barrel wrapped in a piece of cloth to disguise the rough wood.

On October 4, 1904, Mary Bethune stood in the doorway of the Daytona Normal and Industrial School for Training Negro Girls and welcomed her five students with the same smile and warm eyes Miss Emma Wilson had extended to her so many years ago. The dream was no longer just in her heart: It had a street address, some basic equipment and some eager pupils.

Mary had always known that dreams require hard work, and this was no different. What she couldn't solicit for the school, she supplied herself. She sold sweet potato pies to workers and travelers along the railroad. She organized a girls' choir and gave performances at the many fashionable hotels in the city. She continually scrounged all parts of the city for things she could clean and reuse. Every bit of money that came into her hands went into the school. By the end of two years, she had over 200 students and severe overcrowding problems.

A nearby piece of land called "Hell's Hole" caught her eye. It was a city dump; but to Mary Bethune, it was a place where a dream could be built — for $5 down and a little bit of effort. When the junk had been carted off and some makeshift buildings had been put up as temporary classrooms, she began to raise funds for permanent buildings.

Twenty years after these humble beginnings, Mary McLeod Bethune's Daytona school merged with a school for boys in Jacksonville, Florida, to become the Bethune-Cookman Collegiate Institute. The one-time city dump had become a campus with eight buildings, a farm, a twenty-five member faculty and 300 students. The dream born in the heart of a six-year old girl in Mayesville, South Carolina, had come true because of the incredible effort that kept it going. Mary Bethune is a constant reminder to us that a dream is only a dream until determination turns it into reality.

TENACITY ON THE HIGH SEAS

He stood in the open launch hopelessly crowded with nineteen other men and a few supplies, staring at the larger ship receding in the distance. He could still hear the cheers and see the snarling faces of the men who had set them adrift — sailors who had been under his command just that morning. To a dutiful and disciplined captain of His Majesty's Navy, it must have seemed like his worst nightmare come true. His men had mutinied. He knew that more than 3,500 unmapped miles lay between his launch and the nearest friendly shores — just as he knew he and his remaining crew members had little or no chance of surviving.

His captain's eye took stock of his assets: 150 pounds of food; 28 gallons of water; some simple tools; a few swords; sailcloth and rigging; and a sextant, the personal possession of the leader of the mutineers. His liabilities? No maps, no charts, no shelter from sun and sea, no weapons adequate for holding off hostile natives should the sailors choose to search an island for additional food or water.

To anyone else, the situation would look hopeless. To this captain, however, it was just another journey — a rough one, to be sure, and one that would require he employ all his years of expertise to bring his craft and his men to port safely. But — at least in his mind — it *was* achievable. They *would* survive. They *would* make it to safe harbor. They *would* return alive to England. He would see to it. He would make it happen. And so Captain William Bligh took up the most challenging command of his life.

He began by dividing the amount of food and water on hand by the number of days he believed it would take them to reach Timor off the coast of New Holland. He set a rigid ration schedule of one ounce of bread and one cup of water per day, which he enforced for himself as well as his men. If a fish or bird was captured for extra food, it was blindly and impartially distributed among them all. He assigned bailing duties to keep his men exercised. He improved the craft's meager comfort by raising its sides with the sailcloth.

All of his leadership skills were put to the test as the days passed. Doggedly maintaining his role as captain, he doled out chores, made crucial decisions as they arose, defended his rank against the inevitable grousers and commanded his small craft as if it were a British frigate in battle. He made a daily ritual out of charting the craft's speed and distance and kept a journal in anticipation of the day they would step ashore in England. When morale began to flag, he rallied spirits with stories of far-off shores, with memories of England, with words of encouragement and a dose of his own special brandy reserved for just that purpose. And the men gained strength from his strength. The daily discipline, order and routine he enforced became anchors for the wavering hopes of the men under his command.

Miraculously, the craft and its survivors did reach Timor. . . with eleven days of food rations left. In what still stands as one of the most incredible feats of open-boat navigation, Captain William Bligh guided his craft and his men 3,618 miles in 42 days, with the loss of only one life.

This amazing captain of the *H.M.S. Bounty* has gone down in history as the quintessential hard-heart, the ultimate martinet, the abusive authority figure of all time. And perhaps, if we listened only to the mutineers who set him adrift, a case could be made against his coldness, his rigidity, his meanness. But the loyal crewmen he led to safety would certainly have a different perspective. They would see his incredible will and determination as the key factors in their survival. They needed his strength in the face of overwhelming odds to pull them through. The tenacity of one man kept eighteen others alive. For Captain Bligh and the others, *determination* spelled *survival*.

REFLECTIONS ON DETERMINATION...

Some would describe determination as outlasting the opposition. Like the steady drop of water eventually eroding a channel through solid rock or the blade of grass pushing its way through the sidewalk to find the sun, determination is simply the *can* triumphing over the *cannot* through patient, consistent effort. Like Mary Bethune continually scouring trash heaps and baking hundreds of sweet potato pies to make her dream come true.

But there is another side of determination — a flintier aspect. This is the Captain Bligh brand: the teeth-gritting, nose-to-the-grindstone, steely kind of resolve that bends circumstances to one's will and overcomes opposition with pure, unadulterated strength.

Outlasting opposition or overcoming it — quiet, patient effort or powerful, brute force — both speak of the *will* being exerted to accomplish a goal. It's a mark of maturity to live from the will and not from the emotions, to be purposeful in our actions and not be tossed about by whim or changing circumstances.

And it's important to finish well, to refuse to quit in the middle of what we do.

Perhaps what we learn from Mary Bethune and Captain Bligh is that a powerfully directed human will can be both a blessing and a problem. The same determination that makes a dream come true or accomplishes an impossible goal can very easily run roughshod over people if it isn't focused in the right way, on the right things and for the right purpose. It's a difference worth noting.

EXCELLENCE

*Excellence in any department can be attained
only by the labor of a lifetime; it is not
to be purchased at a lesser price.*

— Samuel Johnson

THE "REAL McCOY"

The rhythmic clack of the wheels and the gentle sway of the carriage car were making his fellow travelers sleepy, but young Elijah's thoughts would not stop churning in his head. He was really on his way! He was going to America to work as an engineer on the railroad! The future stretched before him as unendingly bright as the open lands flowing past his window.

His daydreaming faded as he felt the train slowing down for a stop. No depot this time — just another lubricating break. He watched as the fireman/oilman scurried along beside the train, squeezing oil onto all the movable parts, then ran back to restoke the engine. Soon, the train's motion began again.

While his companions settled again into their stupors, Elijah's own "wheels" began to turn again. "There *has* to be a better way to lubricate this train," he mused. "This wastes so much time and money."

Elijah had always thought about the way things worked. Even as a child, he had been fascinated with machines and tools. His father had been careful not to leave anything that could be easily disassembled laying around the farm, because Elijah would quickly take it apart — whether or not he had the knowledge to put it back together again! Yet Elijah's parents never discouraged their son's natural inclinations. They made sure he was given the best education possible, even sending him to Edinburgh, Scotland, to study mechanical engineering. Now, as a master mechanic and engineer, he was on his way to fulfill his dream: He was going to work for the railroad.

As the train finally pulled into Detroit, Elijah was full of hope. But his hopes were soon dashed. He could find no work in his field. No matter that he had graduated from an excellent university in Europe. No matter that he had a degree as a master mechanic and engineer. "His kind" just didn't "make professionals," he was told. The color of his skin was all wrong — Elijah McCoy was a black man. Though the Civil War was over and slavery had been abolished, though he himself had been born free in Canada, the old animosities still governed. He was offered a job on the Central Michigan Railroad as a fireman/oilman — the very job he had so impatiently observed on his journey to Detroit. And because he needed the money, he took it.

The work of a fireman/oilman was backbreaking and dangerous. As the fireman, Elijah had to shovel tons of coal a day into the boiler's furnace so the engine would have a constant supply of steam. As the oilman, he had to run out at every stop, lubricating all the moving parts so they wouldn't seize up. The time-consuming wastefulness of the operation continued to frustrate his mind, even as the exhausting tasks occupied his hands.

Though there were already several devices for continual lubrication on the market, none of them worked very well. For two years Elijah worked at night on his own ideas for a lubricator. He adapted. He refined. He tinkered some more. He started over again. Finally, he was satisfied with what he had done. It was just right. On June 23, 1872, Elijah McCoy was granted a patent from the U.S. Patent Office for his lubricating cup.

At first, Elijah's device was rejected simply because a black man had made it. But his own employers soon saw the superiority of his design and installed his cup on their own engines, under his direct supervision. It was a real turning point for the young inventor. Other engineers saw how efficiently Elijah's model worked and began to install it on their own locomotives. Then steamships crossing the Great Lakes began to use it . . . then the factories of the burgeoning Industrial Revolution. Before too long, no piece of heavy machinery was considered to be in top operating condition without Elijah's model of the lubricating cup.

Inevitably, imitations began to appear. But engineers and mechanics could not be fooled. They refused to use any model but the best, the one marked by excellence of design and craftsmanship. They always asked for Elijah's cup — they demanded "the real McCoy."

Isn't it interesting that the name of this hard-working African-American inventor has become a term we use today to indicate authentic excellence? In his lifetime Elijah McCoy exhibited a continual commitment to excellence in mechanical design. He went on to earn fifty-seven patents, the bulk of them for lubricators of one sort or another. By the early 1920s he had a worldwide reputation for unqualified mechanical genius. But he exhibited a far greater commitment to excellence in *how* he pursued his work. He was never content with second-best efforts, his own or others. Though we remember him for the excellence of his product, the product was only possible because of the excellence of the person who created it. And *that* is an excellence that can be earned by anyone willing to put forth the same effort as the real Elijah McCoy.

OF SOCKS AND SUCCESS

The locker room was filled with the electric excitement of the start of the college basketball season. Nerves...egos...hopes...fears...all were bouncing around the atmosphere like so many charged particles. Just as the anxiety reached the exploding point, the coach entered and began the meeting. You might think his first lesson would be a call to team loyalty, pumping up enthusiasm for his program and the national reputation of the college. But no. This coach — who would ultimately have more national championships to his credit than any other — began by teaching his ambitious, impetuous, up-over-the-rim, in-your-face college basketball players how to put on their socks correctly!

It seemed a leadership style doomed to failure — too many rules, too strict, too outdated. Even *he* admitted that his entire system was exactly what he played in high school! But he wouldn't be dissuaded. He wouldn't let up on his standards. Like the one that prohibited mustaches, goatees or sideburns below the ear lobe and required hair of "reasonable length" (the "reasonableness" to be determined by him and him alone). One year, in fact, three of his star players showed up the day before the first practice, each with some type of violation of his hair rule. He quietly but firmly told them where the clippers and razors were, giving them twenty minutes to decide their basketball futures. And would you believe it — they actually trimmed their hair and played for the man!

He must have been doing *something* right because his system produced some of the best basketball players in the country — players like Kareem-Abdul Jabbar, Bill Walton, Gail Goodrich, Keith Wilkes and Walt Hazzard, to name a few. In his years on the bench, he led UCLA to an unsurpassed ten NCAA National Championships in twelve years, with four of those teams boasting undefeated seasons. Seventeen of the young men he coached were named All Americans a total of twenty-four times; and eleven of his players were first-round NBA draft picks. He is the only man inducted into the Basketball Hall of Fame as both a player and a coach. In a sport increasingly dominated by runaway egos and undisciplined individuality, Coach John Wooden set a standard for team and personal excellence that has never been challenged, let alone equaled. What made the difference for this unassuming man from the basketball-drenched state of Indiana? What made him the coach he was?

In a word, it was *excellence*. Coach Wooden would settle for nothing less than one-hundred percent effort in basketball. And no detail was too small to escape his notice. Shoes and socks were worn just so. Uniforms were worn during practices: No cutoffs or tank tops were allowed to dilute the team identity or work ethic. He even had a rule about how his team left the locker room after games — all tape picked up off the floor, shower heads turned completely off, soap removed, towels all accounted for and left either in the laundry bin or stacked neatly by the door. He planned practices down to the minute and faithfully recorded them in notebooks for future reference. If a player wasn't involved in a five-on-five or three-on-three scrimmage, he was shooting free throws, waiting to be rotated in. The basics were repeated again and again.

His strictness had a motive. He believed passionately that fundamentals were the key: Practice them correctly until they were instinctual and habitual, and the game would take care of itself. It was the little things, he believed, that ultimately made the difference between a champion and a near champion. His goal was to minimize mistakes in those little things so that success could be realized.

But Coach Wooden also pursued excellence in life. Personal habits were just as crucial as basketball skills in the Wooden paradigm. He insisted that his players be self-controlled. They were to dress neatly, keep their rooms orderly and speak politely and courteously at all times. Once he even withdrew a scholarship offer to a potential recruit because he heard the young man speak disrespectfully to his mother. He constantly pressed the young men in his charge to be well-

rounded individuals. He discouraged them from playing basketball in the off-season, both to allow time for
other things and to keep them from picking up slop-
py habits and individualized styles they would have to
undo when the season started!

He was never shy about the moral principles that
guided his life, and he modeled them consistently in
front of his teams. He developed what he called "The
Pyramid of Success," a diagram highlighting some
twenty-five qualities that would lead to success, among
them industriousness, friendship, initiative, self-con-
trol, reliability, honesty and faith. As with basketball, he
believed that if these *life* fundamentals were practiced
diligently and consistently, then success would take
care of itself.

Today John Wooden is recognized for his deep personal commitment to his players as well as his pursuit
of excellence at every level. His philosophy of basketball that produced so many winning seasons and so
many winning human beings was the same as his philosophy for winning in life: Stick with the fundamentals; practice them diligently and consistently until they
are instinctual and habitual; minimize the mistakes in
the small things so that success can be realized. When
it comes right down to it, that's a pretty good definition of excellence no matter what you're doing.

REFLECTIONS ON EXCELLENCE...

When you think of *excellence*, what comes to mind? Do you envision a painting by Monet or a sculpture by DaVinci? Do you hear the notes of Tchaikovsky's *Nutcracker Suite* or Beethoven's *Fifth Symphony* wafting through the air? Do you smell the delicious aroma of Julia Child's French cooking or relive Mary Lou Retton's perfect vault in the Olympics?

Many associate the word with only these kinds of outward manifestations. I don't. I think of it as an *attitude* before it becomes an *action*, a disposition of character that leads to a certain result, not just the result itself. Long before Elijah McCoy's lubricating cup became an excellent piece of work, McCoy himself had laid hold of excellence within, refusing to give up until his invention had taken shape and was the best it could be. Years before John Wooden's UCLA basketball teams achieved unequaled success on and off the court, Wooden himself possessed internal excellence, settling for nothing less than the best from himself before he could expect it from others.

True excellence begins deep inside, with the commitment to bring to bear all of one's resources on an objective, to make the absolute most of everything one has to work with. It is holding to that personal commitment when everyone else is slacking off, taking shortcuts or settling for less just to get by. It is overcoming the deadening tendency toward mediocrity and halfheartedness — giving everything you've got and going for broke. And once you experience it, you will never be the same again.

P E R S I S T E N C E

Let me tell you the secret that has led me to my goal.
My strength lies solely in my tenacity.

— Louis Pasteur

Skeeter's Triumph

Blanch sat by her four-year-old daughter's bed, her eyes brimming with tears. The night air was filled with the sounds of her child's labored breathing...her mother's heart was filled with memories, hopes and fears. There were the memories of little Skeeter's premature arrival in the family, two months early, weighing only four-and-a-half pounds — an enormously threatening birth weight in the 1940s. There were the hopes that the little bundle of energy who survived such an early entry into the world would be able to survive the double pneumonia and scarlet fever assaulting her now. And there were the fears that even if she did survive, the fever would damage her heart and leave her weak for the rest of her life.

"Fight, child," Blanch silently encouraged. "C'mon, you've always been a fighter."

And fight she did. Skeeter survived! But as she struggled to regain her strength, another blow fell. Her left foot began to weaken and twist abnormally to one side. It was polio. The vaccinations we know today had not yet been developed, and polio was the most dreaded disease in the country. Thousands died or were hopelessly crippled in its wake. Skeeter's family was told she would never walk again. The heavy leg brace the doctors strapped around her left leg symbolized all that seemed to drag this young child down.

But Skeeter wasn't the only fighter in her family. Determination ran strong among them. Ed and Blanch were a fiercely independent couple. They had twenty-two children, most of them raised during the Great Depression of the 1930s. Self-reliant and full of love for their offspring, they never gave up. Twice a week, Blanch would take six-year old Skeeter to Meherry Medical College in Nashville. Twice a week, she watched her little girl endure painful therapy that stretched the weakened muscles and strengthened the tendons. Twice a week, she watched the tears of frustration and pain course down her little girl's cheeks. Twice a week, she bundled her little girl home again, to face the same process again in a few days. And twice a week, her mother's strength seemed to work its way into the heart and soul of her child.

Even as she endured all the pain, Skeeter envisioned the day when she would walk again... without the leg brace. How she hated that brace! How it frustrated her! It wasn't just the teasing of the other children... the way they pointed and laughed at her funny walk. It was the *watching* it forced her to do... *watching* others run and play basketball, jump rope and dance... *watching* when she wanted so desperately to be *doing*. In her dreams, though, Skeeter could fly. In her dreams, she was pounding the dirt with her feet, winning race after race. In her dreams, she was dribbling past her older sister and sinking every layup she tried. In her dreams, she was free of everything that hobbled her.

And a competitive, determined fire began to burn in her heart. She would not be beaten. She would walk on her own. She could see it, taste it, feel it!

As the days turned into weeks and weeks into months, Skeeter faithfully did her painful stretching exercises. The brace gave way to a special high-topped shoe. Months turned into years, but she didn't quit. Even when there were no signs of outward progress, she kept on. The fire didn't die.

Four years later, Skeeter enjoyed the first results of her amazing persistence. She walked into church on her own, without the leg brace. This time, the stares, smiles and pointing fingers didn't bother her. This time, she knew the laughter and comments were friendly, not critical or mean. This time, she knew she had won.

It wouldn't be the last time Skeeter would see and hear the affirmations of a crowd. This sickly little child with the hated leg brace grew up to be the first American woman to win three Olympic gold medals and receive the title, "The fastest woman in the world" — Wilma Rudolph.

Wilma "Skeeter" Rudolph was a champion. She faced tremendous physical obstacles and overcame them. But her story is not in the obstacles: Her story is in the overcoming. We all want the victory, the acclaim, the applause. But that kind of greatness isn't achieved overnight. It is the sum of thousands of daily choices to persevere in the face of pain and weariness and despair... to not give up when defeat seems right around the corner... to keep pursuing the goal and be willing to do it one step at a time. Someone once said "triumph" is just some "oomph" added to "try." Skeeter would know all about that!

POOR TOMMY

Poor Tommy. It seemed he never had much of a chance. A sickly child, he never set foot in a school building until he was nearly nine. By then he was so far behind the other children that his teacher pronounced him "addle-brained" and wondered why his parents would even subject him to the torture. He just didn't look well, either. His oddly out-of-proportion head seemed to swivel on his lean, rickety body. And though his hearing was far from keen, he captured enough to send him home in tears and utter frustration. For the next few years, he was schooled at home by his mother, whose confidence and patience soon had him reading Shakespeare and doing basic science experiments in his bedroom.

It was the science that captured his mind and his restless energies. Having learned so much on his own for so long, he was totally at home in the world of observation and experimentation. It was his natural learning style. His first experiment involved trying to hatch goose eggs by sitting on them, just as he'd seen the mother goose do. Then he tried to make a young friend fly by sprinkling him with effervescent powders, supposing the bubbles would raise him aloft. The family cellar became the source of many unusual sounds and smells as Tommy pursued answers to the thousands of questions filling his mind.

When he was twelve, family hardships required that he go to work. The carefree days of mixing powders and liquids with delightful abandon seemed gone forever. But he did learn a few entrepreneurial tricks. While selling snacks on the commuter train between Port Huron and Detroit, Michigan, he acquired a small printing press and produced a daily newspaper for his customers. And he was allowed to set up a laboratory in one of the cars. But even that didn't go well for Tommy. One day he nearly caught the entire car on fire and was summarily ejected from the premises.

His career on the train did have one bright spot, however: He was able to learn how to transmit Morse Code on a telegraph. From the ages of fifteen to eighteen he held and lost perhaps a dozen jobs, excelling in a few, but more frequently getting fired because of his incessant tinkering and fiddling with the already proven and reliable telegraph equipment. And, just as his early teachers probably warned him, he ended up living in run-down flats and rat-infested rooms because he would not (or could not) ply any other trade. Poor Tommy. From the beginning he had seemed doomed to failure. Now he was living it out in spades.

The amazing part was, Tommy didn't even suspect

he was a failure. Instead of listening to his many detractors (a decided advantage of being functionally deaf by this time), he persisted in his love of experimentation and innovation. Then one day he stumbled across Michael Faraday's three-volume *Experimental Researches in Electricity.* At once, his restless mind found its focus. Post-Civil War America was ready for new and radical ideas, especially if they made life easier. And Tommy was ready to explore them all!

His first published invention was the duplex telegraph, which enabled two messages to be sent simultaneously on the same line. Not an earth-shaking discovery, perhaps, but enough of one to gain him a little recognition and some financial backing. Next came his first patent — a vote-recording machine for politicians, replacing the antiquated ballot machines used in Washington. But it was precisely *not* the kind of "improvement" the Washington establishment wanted. From that day forward, Tommy determined that he would never waste his time inventing anything he couldn't sell. He was a new breed — the entrepreneurial inventor!

By 1876, he was ensconced in the Menlo Park, New Jersey, workshop/laboratory that would soon become known around the world for the incredible inventions that poured from its rooms. Here, the relentless urge to investigate, experiment and invent would bring him the title, "The Wizard of Menlo Park." Thomas Alva Edison had finally come into his own. By the end of his life, more than 1,000 patents for successful inventions would be registered in his name.

His famous and much-publicized definition of success — "99% perspiration and 1% inspiration" — revealed a level of persistence that had gone unrecognized for most of his life simply because it had not been expressed in conventional ways. He was creative. He was eccentric. But once an idea got into his head, he would not stop until he had made it successful. His was the persistence of pure, hard work... the long-haul view of things... a brand of "stick-with-it-tive-ness" that our impatient, easily-distracted society could desperately use. Next time you flip on a light switch, think of poor Tommy's hard work... and how much easier your life is because of his persistence. It just might prompt you to roll up your sleeves and get to work.

REFLECTIONS ON PERSISTENCE...

Persistence is the fruit of determination. It is determination in shoe leather, first cousin in a family that specializes in the patience of repeated effort. Persistence doesn't concern itself with how much time passes in reaching a goal — it is concerned only with the goal itself.

Persistence can perform the same task again and again without fretting over monotony or anxiously watching a clock or calendar. Persistence is Wilma Rudolph patiently, doggedly lifting and stretching her twisted limb in thousands of repetitions, day in and day out, until she ultimately could run with abandon. Persistence is Thomas Edison patiently conducting hundreds of experiments with the goal of perfecting one new invention... not bothering to keep track of the failures... his vision fixed solely on the goal of making each innovation the best it could be.

It has been said that the only place where *success* comes before *work* is in the dictionary. Persistence lives by that truth. It outlasts the pain, forgets the failures, refuses the easy way out, never loses sight of the goal. It only has eyes for the prize. Persistence does not quit and it does not die. It just keeps on going until the task is done.

MAGNANIMITY

What I gave, I have; what I spent, I had;
what I kept, I lost.

— Old Epitaph

THE HEART THAT HEALED A NATION

The day had begun with a storm, but the reappearing sun was working its magic on the landscape. The year was 1865 and the location was the Capitol building in Washington, D.C. The people who gathered on that day were weary. They were ready for an end. Their nation had been trapped in the maelstrom of war since they had last assembled here. Could the sunshine of peace be ahead of them at last?

The now-familiar figure of the President-elect rose to the podium . . . tall, bearded, much thinner now and very tired. For four years he had been their leader. For four years he had kept the vision of the Union before the people, enduring a degree of ridicule and vilification no other President has ever encountered, before or since. For four years, he had borne the struggles of a nation at war with itself. The words he spoke that day described the kind of peace he wanted to establish. In their simple eloquence, they set the stage for the kind of healing his countrymen so desperately needed:

"... with malice toward none, with charity for all;

with firmness in the right as God gives us to see the right, let us strive on to finish the work we are in, to bind up the nation's wounds, to care for him who shall have borne the battle and for his widow and his orphan, to do all which may achieve and cherish a just and lasting peace among ourselves and with all nations."

They were words that express the man as no others he ever wrote or spoke. In his plain appearance, straightforward speech and total lack of pretension, he was the quintessential common man. But there was nothing common in his character or his achievements. His was a legacy of greatness that many have tried to emulate, but few have achieved. His name is consistently listed among the most influential leaders of all time. Abraham Lincoln is easily the most revered President in American history.

One would never have believed he was destined for that kind of distinction. Born into abject poverty, he knew only the hardscrabble life of pioneers on the western edge of the early nineteenth-century United States. Creature comforts were few. Work was hard. Not only was he poor: He was uneducated. He often said that his formal education amounted to little less than a year, though he did somehow learn to read, write and multiply through the threes. The first President to be born outside the original thirteen colonies, his was not the refined upbringing that had marked most of the politicians to that date.

And he had not become President on the crest of great personal achievement or notoriety. In fact, he had experienced more failure than success to that point in his life. A business partnership dissolved and he spent seventeen years repaying the debts. He lost more political races than he won, serving only one complete term as a U.S. Congressman some ten years before his presidential candidacy. He was nominated as the least objectionable of the several Republican aspirants in 1860 and was elected with a slim majority of the popular vote only because the Democrats were hopelessly split — not a very auspicious mandate for the leader of a nation on the brink of civil war.

His detractors denounced him as a weak incompetent, totally inadequate for the challenges ahead of him. They ridiculed his appearance, calling him an ape, a baboon, a monster and a clown. But it never provoked a vengeful response. He once stated that he could not afford to act in malice, that what faced him was too important to distort through the lens of personal pettiness. And that largeness of spirit marked his entire Presidency.

When chided for not taking opportunities to destroy his political enemies, he remarked that he felt he destroyed them when he made them his friends. When told that members of his Cabinet, his former political competitors, were touting themselves as far more qualified for the Presidency than he, he heartily agreed and said he wished he could fill his Cabinet with others just like them. When presented with petitions for court-martials and executions for deserters, he either pardoned the men immediately for having "bad legs" that ran away from danger or pigeonholed the requests in his enormous desk, vowing to get to them someday — which he somehow never managed to do.

But the words he spoke at the beginning of his second term offered the clearest statement of that spirit which so characterized his life: "...with malice toward none, with charity for all...." That is the essence of Abraham Lincoln, eloquently distilled. He was never about revenge. It is so fitting that his memorial in Washington, D.C., contains a larger-than-life-size statue of this beloved President. He was larger than life when he was among us. His magnanimous spirit continues to set the example for all of us today.

THE PRICE OF POVERTY

The small figure darting in and out of the doorways looked like a frightened raven seeking shelter from a predator. Her head bobbing from side to side, then back to front, she moved quickly, clothes rustling in her haste to escape the unknown stalker. It was obvious she was poor. You could see it in the clothing — dark and dust-stained, much the worse for wear. You could see it in the features on her face — hard and worn, sharpened by struggles of a sort some could only imagine.

Poverty can do strange things to people. Reduced circumstances can reduce human beings to behaviors and feelings they never imagined before. But so can wealth. Contrary to appearances, it was not an insolvent beggar ducking in and out of the doorways of New York City. It was Hetty Green, a genius in the Wall Street world of shrewdness and financial acumen of the 1800s.

Raised in a wealthy businessman's home, Hetty was able to read the *New York Times* financial pages by the age of six. She inherited a $4.8 million family estate at the age of thirty and became a real "mover and shaker" in the world of stocks, bonds, securities and cash. Everything she touched yielded dividends and gains. Before too long, her cash operating balance at the bank exceeded $2 million, with an annual family income estimated at $3 million.

But you would never know it by the way she lived. Her carriage — when she used one — had once been a chicken roost. She refused an office, choosing instead to work on the floor of her bank, surrounded by boxes and chests of her papers. Her life was an endless succession of dingy rooms, cheap meals and unwashed clothes. Moving her family from place to place to avoid paying property taxes, her children never enjoyed the security their mother's wealth could have provided. When her son suffered a leg injury and they were recognized and asked to pay at a clinic for the indigent, she refused and treated the injury herself, resulting in eventual infection and amputation of the boy's leg. She also suffered from constant paranoia. Convinced that the next person on the street might be a murderer or thief, she was constantly on the lookout for imaginary stalkers. She died of a stroke while arguing over the price of milk.

Immeasurable wealth, incredible financial prowess, an extravagant income guaranteed for life — yet Hetty Green chose to live as a miser and forced her children into deprivation. Why would anyone choose to live like a pauper with immense wealth literally at hand?

Some would blame it on *greed* — an affection for material wealth that overpowers every other aspect of our character. It is, as one person has described it, an unnatural obsession with financial gain, to the exclusion of every personal virtue. The old-fashioned word is "covetousness." It corrupts everyone in whom it finds a home. And like a cancerous tumor, it grows to eventually consume its host.

In another sense, greed is nothing more than a distinct form of poverty — a poverty not of the purse, but of the person. Though rich in all the ways Wall Street deemed rich, Hetty Green was a pauper in her soul. One of the takers, the gatherers, the hoarders, she never seemed to have enough. The more she gained, the more she wanted. The more she wanted, the more miserly she became. In spite of her incredible wealth, hers was the legacy of diminished returns of the spirit.

The cure for this kind of self-consuming misery? A healthy mix of contentment and thankfulness, with a dose of generosity for good measure. To use what we have wisely and to share it with joy is one of the greatest secrets of human happiness. It is guaranteed to keep us from the poverty that kills the soul.

REFLECTIONS ON MAGNANIMITY...

Two more contrasting characters would be hard to find. Their life experiences would fall at opposite ends of whatever scale you might choose. Poverty — privilege. Disappointment — success. Yet their lives reveal an astonishing reversal of attitudes. One would expect Lincoln to have grown the hard outer shell, to have developed a deep cynicism and suspicion of the human race. But it was the sheltered, advantaged Hetty Green who has gone down in history as the bitter recluse, the shriveled soul who found no happiness or satisfaction in the abundance that came her way.

No difference in gender, temperament or personal style can explain the difference. No element of circumstance or life situation can be determined as the root cause. The only conclusion that can be drawn is that the spirit we develop in our lives is not a matter of genes or environment — it is a matter of choice and choice alone. At any time, either of these two people could have acted in the opposite manner. Lincoln could have started keeping track of the slights, the outright ridicule, the calculated opposition. He could have become self-protective, "victimized" in his thinking, vengeful. Hetty Green could have relaxed her iron-fisted grip on her wealth, loosened up a bit and not died in a paroxysm over pennies. But they *chose* not to. And those choices shaped the spirit that would characterize their lives.

It is an undeniable principle: We can't always control what life brings us, but we can control how we respond to it. We can choose to be made *better* or *bitter* by what comes our way.

Two portraits hang on the wall of history for your perusal: the magnanimous Lincoln and the miserable Green. Whom you choose to be like is up to you . . . and you alone.

DILIGENCE

Great occasions do not make heroes or cowards; they simply unveil them. Silently and imperceptibly, as we wake or sleep, we grow strong or weak; and at last some crisis shows what we have become.

— Brooke Foss Westcott

THE MAKING OF A MAESTRO

The crowd was in an absolute uproar. People were on their feet shouting angry insults, shaking their fists and stomping their feet in rage. How dare this miserable group of foreigners arrive in their country and insult them like this! Wave after wave of catcalls filled the air. Jeers, taunts and hoots of ridicule rebounded off the ceiling, seeming to gain force with each repetition.

But this wasn't the typical pandemonium of a modern hockey game or rock concert. This was the stately Imperial Theater in Rio de Janeiro in June of 1886. The crowd was a culturally sophisticated and normally quite civil group of upper-class socialites. And the event was...an opera!

The tension had been brewing since the tour began. The Italian orchestra normally toured South America during the off-season and had graciously allowed its only Brazilian member to serve as conductor. But his arrogant manner and perceived musical inferiority had become increasingly sore spots for the performers. The lackluster opening performance in Rio the night before had been the last straw. When even the Brazilian papers criticized the conductor's leadership, the orchestra organizers replaced him with his Italian assistant. The Brazilian publicly quit in disgust, claiming that the Italians were horrible performers who failed to follow his direction. The Italians countered with charges of his utter incompetence. That was all it took to ignite the nationalistic passions of his Brazilian compatriots. And the elegant Imperial Theater was literally shaking with their response. First, they shouted the replacement Italian conductor off the stage. Then the chorus master was drafted and took his place to start the overture — but he dropped the baton and fled the orchestra pit before a note was sounded.

What to do? To call off the performance meant ending the season, stranding the entire group in South America without adequate funds to return to Europe. But it also meant confessing they were incapable of performing — and this they could not do.

Members of the troupe approached the organizer with their final hope: Let the first cellist lead the orchestra. He had been helping the chorus to rehearse. He knew the scores, even better than some of them did. But the first cellist was a young nineteen-year old, fresh out of music school on his first tour. In desperation, the organizer agreed. But how could this *bambino* possibly know what he was doing?

He could know because of how he had spent the

last ten years of his life. Born in Parma, Italy, it was simply understood that the young man would grow up knowing and loving opera — it was the common music of the day. And so it was not considered unusual that he had learned many of the aria melodies by the time he started school. An astute teacher first observed his tremendous ability to memorize. When she discovered he also had an awareness beyond the ordinary in music, she recommended musical training. Though it was a real financial hardship for the family, he began to attend the Royal School of Music when he was nine years old. He made the most of the opportunity. The dreary, almost monastic environment of the school did nothing to quench his dream of becoming a musician. He was determined to excel, no matter what the sacrifice. While other students were concentrating on just one instrument, he was mastering two: the cello and the piano. When others contented themselves with studying only the musical scores found in the conservatory library, he found ingenious ways to obtain new ones, even selling his meat-ration coupons to less farsighted friends to earn the needed funds. For ten years, he had been totally focused on preparing for his career as a musician. Now, one year after graduating with top honors, all that preparation was being put to the test.

The young man stepped into the orchestra pit and the crowd quieted somewhat, as if appraising their next victim. Then they began to laugh. Was this all the Italians had left to offer? The young man strode to the podium and glared the audience into silence. Angrily, almost defiantly, he raised his baton; and with his emphatic downbeat, the orchestra triumphantly blasted the first notes of *Aïda*. The audience settled back in quiet curiosity. The young cellist was directing with such fire and enthusiasm that the opera came alive. All the years of quiet, lonely preparation in that dreary boarding school in Parma were now flowing out from him and lavishly spilling over on all who heard him. All the hours spent studying the musical scores, his stomach rumbling with hunger, found their fruition in the rich tapestry of sound that blanketed that Brazilian opera house.

As the final curtain rang down, there was a momentary stunned silence, then thunderous applause. The world had just lost a first cellist and gained a maestro — the incredible Arturo Toscanini.

Many tried to explain Arturo Toscanini's "instant success." They attempted to attribute it to his incredible memory and extraordinary natural talent. They spoke of his extraordinary "luck" at being in the right place at the right time. The fact of the matter is, Arturo's success was not instant. Nor was it even due primarily to his giftedness or his placement in the scope of history. Arturo had labored and prepared for ten long, hard years, enduring obscurity, sacrificing personal pleasure and doing far more than was expected in order to reach that "pinnacle of fame" in Rio de Janeiro. The moment that catapulted him into world consciousness could just as easily have marked him as a pretender, an incompetent, a hopeless failure. But when the moment came, he was ready. He had been diligently, quietly preparing for it for more than a decade. It all came together because he was altogether prepared.

WHAT IF?

The men and matériel had been mobilized for weeks. New runways had been constructed on the flight's termination point. An experimental direction finder had been installed on the site as a backup. Three ships — two Navy and one Coast Guard — had been stationed in strategic points along the flight path to monitor the plane's position and safety. And on the morning of July 2, 1937, the tension in the various locales was near the breaking point. For eighteen hours, men in the Coast Guard cutter *Itasca* had been hunched over their receivers, listening for transmissions from the pilot of the flight. They had run the range of frequencies, hearing tantalizing bits of communication from the airplane, only to lose them before a fix could be taken. And what they had heard had not been encouraging. There had been repeated requests for current weather information, which had been duly transmitted, but never acknowledged. There had been instructions to transmit location signals on ever-changing frequencies, frequencies that made no sense to the radio operators. There had been whistles into the microphone to provide location, but the whistles only came through as static to the sailors.

At 8:45 A.M. the last transmission was received: an incomplete bearing and the ominous report that fuel was running low with still no sight of land. A massive search was launched, involving seven Navy ships over a period of seventeen days covering 250,000 square miles of ocean. But no one ever heard from the pilot again. Amelia Earhart — "Lady Lindy" — the famed female aviatrix of the 1930s — was lost.

It was a story that gripped the globe. Amelia Earhart had caught the fancy of the prewar world as no other woman had. In 1928, she had been the first female to cross the Atlantic in an airplane. And though she had just been a passenger on that flight, she received most of the publicity, bringing her financial backing and notoriety in an arena where women had never been before. In 1932, she followed in the footsteps of Charles Lindbergh, becoming the first woman to fly a plane solo across the Atlantic. In 1935, she made the first solo flight from Honolulu to the American mainland and the first nonstop flight from Mexico City to Newark, New Jersey. She was feted in parades, spoke on lecture tours, even touted her own line of luggage. In the hands of her media-savvy husband, she was a marketing marvel before the age of Madison Avenue.

The flight around the world in 1937 was to be the culmination of her career. But from the beginning, plans for the flight were marred by inconsistencies, poor planning and lack of foresight. She chose as her navigator a man with a tremendous reputation for celestial navigation — and a debilitating alcohol problem. She refused several offers of mechanical and technical help from sources along the route of her path, even turning down the offer of a tuning crystal from Pan American Airways that would have enabled ground stations to track her at regular intervals during the flight.

And the radios were a constant source of frustration. Something always seemed to be going wrong with them. Minimalists at best when it came to equipment, both Amelia and her navigator showed a frightening disregard for the crucial role of communication in their task. Neither knew Morse Code or bothered to learn even the rudimentary techniques of key transmission. In fact, they purposefully left their Morse Code key and a 250-foot trailing wire antenna on the ground in Miami, either of which would have provided a much more constant locating signal than voice communications... either of which might have made the difference in what eventually transpired.

On the morning of July 1, 1937, Amelia stood poised on the Western edge of the Pacific for the last legs of her flight. She had already flown over 20,000 miles in little over a month, making thirty stops in nineteen countries. Some 7,000 miles lay between her and landfall in Oakland, California. But this leg — from Lae, New Guinea, to tiny Howland Island in the

Pacific Ocean — was undoubtedly the most dangerous. Howland Island is a two-by-one-half-mile speck
in the vast waters of the Pacific. And Amelia and her
navigator had to find it within eighteen hours of their
takeoff.

All the preparations that others could make for her
had been made. The three ships, the extra direction
finder, the new runways — all were in order and waiting her arrival. But the preparations Amelia herself had
failed to make would keep her from a safe landfall. In
neglecting to consider every eventuality — she
neglected everything. She counted on clear weather
for navigating — and ran into squalls and overcast
skies. She counted on her navigator's skills to keep her
on course — and more than once had to load him
onto the plane in a drunken stupor. She counted on
chronometers for nighttime navigating — and they
were never set properly. She counted on her shorter
antenna to carry her signals — and found it incapable
of reaching the stations she needed to contact. She
counted on her own knowledge of radio — and discovered it totally inadequate for the conditions she
faced. Her lack of foresight and almost casual attitude
toward the demands of the trip are hard to understand. But the result is no surprise at all. In failing to
prepare, Amelia Earhart prepared to fail. Not purposefully, not consciously... but nonetheless in reality.

In all the questions that surround any such calami-
tous situation, one can only ask, "*What if* she had

learned Morse Code and kept the key on board? *What if* she had not abandoned the longer trailing antenna that would have transmitted her signal long enough for a fix to be taken on her position? *What if* she had checked more closely the frequencies necessary to communicate with the *Itasca?*"

What if she had done *any* of the things she left undone? The headlines in July of 1937 might have been totally different — and the world would still be celebrating her victory instead of mourning her loss.

REFLECTIONS ON DILIGENCE...

Diligence relates to detail as persistence relates to time: It knows no limit. The diligent person pays painstaking attention to every element of his duty, to every facet of the task at hand. Less conscientious types might call it "perfectionism" or even "paranoia."

"Lighten up!" they'd say. "Go with the flow, man. You can't possibly think of everything. Relax! It'll all work out!"

Diligence has no ears for the siren song of slackness. It lives by the rule of "one more time" — one more time through the checklist, one more time over the music, one more reading of the manuscript. In essence, it is the discipline of carefulness: carefulness in preparation, carefulness in execution. Amelia Earhart's tragic failure was nothing more — or less —

than a lack of attention to those bothersome little details that seemed unnecessary or that somehow detracted from the limelight, from the pursuit of a moment's fame. By contrast, Toscanini's famous debut that night in Buenos Aires was successful only because he had spent years of solitary, careful diligence preparing for that success. He never knew when or if it would come, but he was ready nonetheless.

Benjamin Franklin wisely reminds us of the power of little things in large outcomes:

> For the want of a nail the shoe was lost,
> For the want of a shoe the horse was lost,
> For the want of a horse the rider was lost,
> For the want of a rider the battle was lost,
> For the want of a battle the kingdom was lost,
> And all for the want of a horse-shoe nail.

Watch the little things. They can make a bigger difference than you might imagine.

COMPASSION

Compassion is your pain in my heart.

— Anonymous

WHERE AN ANGEL DARED TO TREAD

Clara Barton surveyed the scene before her and her heart sank. Not even noon yet and already more than 300 wounded soldiers lay around the barn groaning, bleeding, dying. The smoke and hot backlash of the artillery fire began to fill her eyes and burn her face. Gathering the food and medicine she had brought, she headed toward the mangled men she had come to serve. As she knelt by each one in turn, she was glad she had slipped ahead of her assigned place in the army supply train to arrive early. She was glad, too, for the lessons she had learned at Cedar Mountain, Bull Run and Chantilly. This time, she was better prepared. This time, she could do more to ease the incredible suffering of the men who were fighting.

And it was a good thing. This was Antietam on September 17, 1862 — soon to be the bloodiest single day in the entire Civil War.

Clara Barton had been gathering supplies for the Union soldiers and treating their wounded since the war began in April, 1861. She had been appalled at

how the injured men arrived at the hospital in
Washington, D.C., many of them days after the battles... wounds caked with dirt and blood ... throats
parched from lack of water. She had seen the waste —
the hundreds of men who died on the way, not from
their injuries but from infection and dehydration. She
could not accept the unnecessary suffering she saw. She
could not understand why the men had to wait days to
be treated. She began petitioning the Secretary of War
early in 1862 to allow her to go to the battlefield itself
with food, medicine and supplies that she would gath-
er and transport. It took her until August to gain per-
mission to go.

Once cleared, she wasted no time. Her first experience on an actual battlefield was Cedar Mountain in
Virginia. Arriving four days after the conflict, she
found the area still full of wounded, Union and
Confederate alike, many of them just hours away from
death. For five days and nights, she moved among the
men, offering a soft touch on the face or a comforting
word. She cleaned their wounds as best she could. She
replaced their torn uniforms with fresh shirts or blankets to keep them warm. She fed them all, distributing
every bit of donated food she had collected.

Just a few days later, she cared for almost 3,000
men at the Second Battle of Bull Run. Then at
Chantilly, she worked through a torrential rain that
accompanied the battle, climbing from wagon to
wagon to feed and comfort the wounded — some of
whom had already lain on the battlefield for three days

before arriving at the train station for transport to the hospitals. She refused to leave until the last men were safely on the trains, escaping herself only minutes ahead of the invading enemy cavalry.

These three battles within days of each other convinced Clara that she needed to "follow the cannon" and be at the battles from the beginning. It did the men little good for her to arrive days after they were wounded. So many who could have been saved with a little primary care and some simple nourishment had needlessly perished. And the three battles showed the military commanders that this small, slender forty-year old woman knew what she was doing. So it was that Clara arrived at Antietam with her own army wagon of supplies and her own drivers, just as the most horrific battle of the Civil War was beginning.

For much of the next two years, Clara continued to "follow the cannon" in Virginia, Maryland, Pennsylvania and even South Carolina. Wherever she went, she brought light and comfort to those she touched. It may have been as simple as a biscuit or a drink of water, a hard-boiled egg or a cup of applesauce. It may have been nothing more than moving a man gently into a more comfortable position, making him warmer with a blanket or a covering of hay. It may have been a whispered promise to a dying young man to tell his mother he loved her and he died well. Whatever the need, she was there. The men called her the "Angel of the Battlefield."

When the war was over, Clara turned her attention

to another group of wounded: those left behind by the fighting. She began an Office of Correspondence to find and identify many of the missing men for their anguished families. In the first four years after the war, she and her assistants personally wrote over 100,000 letters, seeking and sharing information, much of it at her own expense. They scoured hospital and prison records for names and dates of wounded and dead. She personally went to the notorious Andersonville prison in Georgia and helped to properly identify and re-inter the remains of nearly all the 13,000 Union soldiers who had died there. All in all, over 22,000 families received information about their husbands, sons and brothers because of Clara Barton.

Near collapse, Clara was sent to Europe in 1869 to rest. There, she was introduced to the International Convention of Geneva, a society formed in 1865 to help lessen the sufferings of war. Among other things, the ten articles of the Geneva Convention provided for complete neutrality for all hospitals, hospital personnel and medical supplies in time of war. The organization adopted a red cross on a white background as their international symbol and became more popularly known as The Red Cross. Clara spent much of the next twelve years trying to persuade her country to adopt the Geneva Convention and become one of the nations committed to this kind of humanitarian relief. It took her until 1882. Clara established the first chapters of the Red Cross in the U.S. and served as president of the American organization until 1904, when she was 90 years old.

Today, the name Clara Barton is almost synonymous with *compassion*...the ability to suffer with another. She could not turn away from the wounded young soldier, the grieving mother or the orphaned child. Their needs moved her heart and then her hands. For over fifty years, Clara Barton dedicated herself to relieving suffering wherever she encountered it. She is a constant reminder to us that feeling the pain of others is not enough — we must share in the suffering enough to do something about it.

THE REAL SCORE

He arrived for football camp in the oppressive heat of August. Since childhood he had dreamed of playing football. The dream began many chilly autumn nights before when he and his Dad watched his beloved Wildcats face another challenger. As a boy he longed for the day he, too, would wear the Green and the Gold and would hear his name announced over the public address system to the roar of the crowd. Though never a "star" or the "best" on any of his teams, he worked hard, maintained an honor student ranking, even started on both offense and defense in his junior year. Noticed by recruiters in his senior year, he received scholarship offers from several Division 1 schools. The day he signed his letter of intent was one of the most exciting in his life. Now he was here — college football camp — and it was incredible!

As the two weeks of practice drew to a close, self-doubt and physical exhaustion began to take their toll. Every player there was as good or better than he had ever hoped to be. But by two weeks into the season, he had worked his way onto the traveling squad and was being placed on specialty teams. Hope began to return. Then the injury occurred: a devastating ankle sprain. The season was lost!

A greater loss was occurring off the field, though. His grades were suffering terribly. He completed his first semester passing only six credit hours. Second semester started in late January. Winter workouts for football began in mid-February. While walking to his last winter workout before spring practice began, he stared blankly at his midterm grades: C-F-F-F-F. He had failed four out of five midterm exams.

Failed. He withered under the awful weight of the word. Fear, despair and discouragement rushed in with their mocking voices, reminding him gleefully of his shortcomings. After all, the failure wasn't caused by someone or something else: It was his own lack of preparation and effort. He had only himself to blame.

His mind racing, he turned to the one activity in which he had at least minimal success — physical exertion. He lifted weights and ran during that workout as if exercise could solve his other problems. But it only added physical exhaustion to the mental and emotional exhaustion he was already feeling.

At the end of the workout, he sat on the bottom steps leading out of the gym, his head cradled in his hands. He could hear his teammates and others laughing and discussing their plans as they left. His sense of isolation was quickly growing into self-pity. "How could I have gotten here?" "What will my folks say?"

"I'm nothing but a failure."

His thoughts were interrupted by the sound of footsteps. Aware that the steps had ceased, he felt an arm go around his shoulder. Surprised, the young athlete stiffened and quickly turned to see who was there. The concern etched on the face of one of his coaches spoke volumes to the young man.

Coach Lou Tepper was the Defensive Coordinator. A bundle of enthusiasm, he was respected for his knowledge and ability to encourage the young men on his teams. He knew well the situation at hand. In typical fashion, he was very direct.

"You don't think you're going to make it, do you, son?" he inquired.

Overwhelmed, the young player could not control his emotions. He began to sob. Fighting to gain his composure, the only words he could mutter were, "No, sir, I don't."

Determined to make eye contact, Coach Tepper emphatically stated, "Well, I do — and I believe in you!"

The conversation was over in thirty seconds. With a firm squeeze to the shoulder, Lou Tepper left the young man with those words ringing in his ears, "Well, I do — and I believe in you!"

How can a few words of encouragement really make that much of a difference? How can a simple act of concern and kindness really matter? Well, they do; and it does. Encouragement is a powerful antidote to the snakebite of failure.

Years later, when the Coach and player were visiting, the player wanted to express his gratitude for the encouragement he had received years earlier. As he related the story, a blank look came over the Coach's face.

"You do remember, don't you, Coach?" asked the former player.

Embarrassed to admit it, he nevertheless replied honestly, "No, I'm sorry, I don't."

Of course he didn't remember. The act that was life-changing for the former player had been repeated so often that for the Coach, it was simply "life."

Lou Tepper continues to coach college football today. Beyond the percentages continuing to accumulate in the stat books, there is one young man among hundreds who already knows the real score: Lou Tepper is a winner.

As for our young player? In the strength of his coach's words, the young man did make it. He completed his football career as a three-year starter. He graduated from college in the prescribed four years by attending summer school. He went on to earn a Masters Degree in counseling so he could do for others what Lou Tepper had done for him. Today he teaches seminars around the country encouraging young and old alike to develop character and moral strength. And you hold his book in your hands.

Reflections on Compassion . . .

Compassion is one of the most beautiful words in the English language — and one of the most misunderstood. Many think they experience compassion when their hearts are momentarily stirred to pity by what they see on the television or bump into on the street. But the word literally means "to suffer with," to so identify with another's pain that it becomes *your* pain. Far more than a fleeting emotional blip on the screen of our lives, it is *passion* turned into *action*. It is not just being *moved by* something, but *moving out to do* something.

Clara Barton knew the difference. She wasn't just touched by the suffering of others — she moved out to do something to change it. Her compassion was expressed in literal cups of cold water, pieces of bread, blankets and medicines. One could almost take inventory of her passion as it took action. Thousands lived because of how she suffered with them.

Lou Tepper's compassion for the hurting young

athlete he saw on the steps that evening was no less life-giving. His passion, his joining in my suffering, motivated him to simply speak a few words of encouragement. But they were words that changed my life.

Someone once said that the smallest deed is better than the greatest intention. That's compassion in a nutshell: doing something to relieve the suffering of another. Around us exists a hurting world, filled with people waiting for a touch from someone. That touch may mean the difference between hope and defeat, between life and death. Will you put your passion into action today?

M O R A L I T Y

To keep clear of concealment, to keep clear of the need of concealment, to do nothing that he might not do out on the middle of Boston Common at noonday — I cannot say how more and more that seems to me to be the glory of a young man's life. It is an awful hour when the first necessity of hiding anything comes. The whole life is different thenceforth. When there are questions to be feared and eyes to be avoided and subjects that must not be touched, then the bloom of life is gone. Put off that day as long as possible. Put it off forever if you can.

— Philipps Brooks

Through the Eyes of a Child

What does it take to become a great author? Some aspire to it from childhood. Some pursue it as a career choice, others as an expression of their creativity. In the often cutthroat world of publishing, only the strong survive and become the "prominent," the writers of renown, those whose books are accurately called "the classics."

But one particular young author was not of this mold. Lovingly nicknamed "Mrs. Quackenbush" by a teacher because of her girlish delight in chattering in school, she thought *maybe* she could be a journalist someday, since she enjoyed the act of writing — but not a world-renowned writer of nonfiction, though that is exactly what her book made her.

Her writing was not bad, mind you, but it was hardly the stuff that would merit literary success today. Instead of penning unabashed ramblings about sex, "Mrs. Quackenbush" wrote about a first kiss, a growing romance, the strange new feelings of a first love. Instead of punctuating her writing with stories of deceit and personal power, she wrote about friendship and trust.

Mostly her writing was composed of her day-by-day conversation with a close friend — perhaps her closest friend — named Kitty. They were words of youth, of wide-eyed observations of the world. Not that her life did not offer its own frustrations, disappointments, even deep disillusionment, particularly as she grew older. There was much about her world that troubled and mystified her — yet she could write even about these things with a naïveté that intuitively expected the best from herself, from her friends, from her family, even from strangers.

Perhaps, then, it is "Mrs. Quackenbush's" unquenchable spirit of optimism, her belief in the human heart's innate thirst for goodness that has kept her book alive for so long and has spread its vicarious message to so many. To date it has far surpassed twenty million copies and has been translated into more than fifty-five languages. It is regarded as something even beyond a classic, really — more of a first-person treatise on what is best, as well as what may be worst, in the human heart. All from someone who never aspired to be a great author at all.

Her only work, in fact, was this record of messages to Kitty; and it was very much an unfinished story. The final words she penned were simply a heartfelt vow to keep on trying to become what she wanted to be in spite of other people in the world. Unfortunately for "Mrs. Quackenbush" there were other people living in the world. And on August 4, 1944, they came for her.

Bursting into the hidden "annex" adjoining a factory in Amsterdam, the Nazi SS police took Otto Frank, his Jewish friends and Jewish family — including their fifteen-year-old daughter, Anne — from their secret hideaway, leaving behind their ransacked personal belongings. Among those belongings was Anne's diary, which she had lovingly named "Kitty." And though the irrepressible "Mrs. Quackenbush" and all her family except her father died in the squalid brutality of Nazi concentration camps, *The Diary of Anne Frank* lives on today as a legacy of pure unworldliness, as well as a haunting reminder of the way purity itself views the ultimate expression of evil.

Of all that perished in the ashes of Word War II, Anne Frank warns us against perhaps the greatest loss of all: the loss of personal innocence. To see great evil is a horrendous thing. To choose to participate in it, even worse. To remain pure and uncorrupted even as one suffers in a world of unspeakable lawlessness is perhaps the greatest achievement of all. Somehow, a fifteen-year old child in Germany managed to show us that it is not an impossible task.

LESSONS FROM PARADISE

It wasn't supposed to end like this. This was supposed to be paradise — the enjoyment of complete, unrestricted freedom. No rules. No routines. No expectations beyond pleasure. Instead, there was absolute disillusionment. Destruction. Death. The two British sailors surveyed the grim ruggedness of their island home and the remnants of its shattered society in despair. How had it gone so wrong?

It had begun with such promise. Actually, it had started with a rebellion; but to the overworked sailors of the *H.M.S. Bounty*, mutiny had seemed the only way out. Once rid of their tyrannical captain and his repeated humiliations, they were free to return to the sun-washed shores and beautiful women of Tahiti they had so recently enjoyed. For several weeks they drank deeply of the unfettered relaxation and unrestrained sexual pleasure of the South Sea island. But then the reality of their capital crime began to sink in. Fearing for their lives, nine of them sailed from Tahiti with eighteen Tahitians — twelve of them women —

in search of a hiding place. Four long months later, they came to the uncharted, uninhabited island of Pitcairn, burned the *Bounty* to hide evidence of their presence and started their own society from scratch. It was to be a society based on unbridled freedom. Pure enjoyment. Absolute pleasure. *Pitcairn* spelled *paradise* to these beleaguered seekers.

But the glow didn't last long. Resentment began to brew as the nine British sailors took one woman each for themselves, leaving only three women for the six Tahitians. When two of the white sailors' women died, they kidnapped two of the remaining Tahitian women to replace them. The hostility erupted into the open as the Tahitian men tried to murder the sailors and ended up losing two of their own. Barely a year into their new society, they had experienced racial discrimination, kidnapping, rape, conspiracy and murder — all in the land of "perfect freedom."

Within another five years, only two of the original mutineers were left. They had seen six of their companions murdered and watched a seventh take his life in utter alcoholic despair. All the Tahitian men had been killed. One of the Tahitian women had committed suicide. The original landing party of twenty-seven had been reduced to the two of them, a handful of women and their half-Tahitian, half-English offspring.

No, it wasn't supposed to end like this. The freedom that had held such promise had brought only dissipation and destruction. The future looked as grim as the jagged rocks of their island home. Pitcairn no longer spelled *pleasure*. It spelled *prison*.

It was then that they made the discovery. One of the mutineers had brought a Bible off the *Bounty* before it was burned. No one had paid any attention to it before, but the desperate men had no other source of hope. Having experienced firsthand the bankruptcy of unbridled human nature, they had no problem in accepting its truths about man and God. They had no problem in accepting their accountability to operate by standards higher and nobler than theirs had been. So they began to read the Book, earnestly and deliberately. They began to pray and instruct their children in the simple precepts and disciplines that have brought order and true liberty to every society that has applied them.

And Pitcairn was transformed. Today, though the island's population has been culled and many have moved away, those that remain live lives marked by a distinct faith, by discipline, integrity and simplicity — all undergirded by a strong sense of personal responsibility to God and to each other.

Amazing, isn't it, that freedom wouldn't come from the *lack* of restraint, but from its *practice?* Astounding, don't you think, in a world gone drunk on libertarianism and hedonism, that a sense of personal and communal accountability could be the key to a healthy society? In our "anything goes" world of self-indulgent excess, could it possibly be that we need to rediscover what those desperate people on Pitcairn Island did so many years ago? Our survival — like theirs — could be at stake. It might be worth a look.

REFLECTIONS ON MORALITY. . .

In our modern society of revisionist thinking and free expression, you would be hard pressed to find a topic less popular than this one. Why? Because any mention of morality automatically demands that we talk about right and wrong. Good and evil. Acceptable and unacceptable. Standards that people should abide by or suffer negative consequences. It means drawing a line in the sand and saying, "I will go no farther." It means acknowledging the existence of moral absolutes in a world caught in the tailspin of relativism and unqualified tolerance.

No wonder it is so unpopular. And if you want to know how unpopular even a discussion of morality is today, just try standing in front of a group of people and disagreeing with certain behaviors or lifestyles.

Regardless, we can only avoid the subject for so long. Sooner or later we must talk about it. We must again find our voices and discuss the things that really matter. We must stand for what is right and stand against what is wrong. We must fall in love with innocence, decency and integrity. If we are to experience the best life has to offer, we must face down the worst it brings out in some people. And if we hope to ever see a renewed national virtue, that process must begin with renewed personal virtue.

French historian Alexis de Tocqueville came to America to explore the secret of her greatness. His search led him to the following observation:

> "America is great because America is good;
> and when America ceases to be good,
> America will cease to be great."

Enough said.

INDEX OF
CHARACTER PROFILES

Adams, John Quincy............37

Barton, Clara............127

Bethune, Mary McLeod 61

Bligh, Captain William 67

Bounty Mutineers 145

Carawan, Gladys............3

Carver, George Washington 9

Custer, George Armstrong............15

Earhart, Amelia............117

Edison, Thomas Alva 91

Frank, Anne............141

Green, Hetty............103

Lee, Robert E............25

Liddell, Eric............29

Lincoln, Abraham............99

McCoy, Elijah............75

Navajo Code-Talkers............49

Rudolph, Wilma............87

Soicho, Yokoi 53

Tepper, Lou............133

Toscanini, Arturo............111

Tubman, Harriet............41

Wooden, John 79

FOR FURTHER INFORMATION

A powerful and dynamic speaker, Rolfe Carawan travels over one-hundred days a year delighting young and old alike with his humor and captivating illustrations.

He is widely known for his innovative presentations addressing the need for personal and corporate character in every aspect of our lives.

If you would like Rolfe to address your business, association, nonprofit organization, school or church, please contact us at:

LIFEMATTERS INTERNATIONAL
1-800-258-3966

To order additional copies of

Profiles In Character

Please send _____ copy(ies)
    at $19.95 for each copy   = $ _____

plus $3.50 shipping and
    handling for each book   = $ _____

WA residents add 8.2% tax   = $ _____

Enclosed is my check
    or money order for   = $ _____

Please send my books to:

Name _____

Address _____

City _____ State _____ Zip _____

Phone _____

Return this order form to:

LifeMatters International
31308 41st Pl. SW
Federal Way, WA 98023
1-800-258-3966